Norfolk
MURDERS

Norfolk
MURDERS

NEIL R. STOREY

The
History
Press

First published in the United Kingdom in 2006 by Sutton Publishing Limited

Reprinted in 2009 by
The History Press
The Mill, Brimscombe Port,
Stroud, Gloucestershire, GL5 2QG
www.thehistorypress.co.uk

British Library Cataloguing in Publication Data
A catalogue record for this book is available from the British Library.

ISBN 978-0-7509-4366-6

*To ex-Chief Inspector Alan Chapman
of Norfolk Constabulary, a fine
copper and a good friend.*

Typeset in 10.5/13.5pt Sabon.
Typesetting and origination by
Sutton Publishing Limited.
Printed and bound in England by
Athenaeum Press Ltd.

CONTENTS

Norwich Castle, *c.* 1875. Hangings drew large crowds. On execution days the scaffold was usually erected between the gatehouses and the concourse over the cattle market.

ACKNOWLEDGEMENTS

I have been granted privileged access to numerous public and private archives and collections in the preparation of this book, and so to all – too numerous to mention – who have opened their doors to me, I say a genuine thank you. It has been proved, yet again, that when researching some of the darkest tales from Norfolk's past, I have met and renewed the acquaintance of some of the nicest people.

I am also grateful for the kind and fascinating letters, compliments, and snippets of information, I have received from readers of my regular 'Grisly Tales' features in the *Norfolk Journal*. Naturally, I wish to extend my thanks to all of them, but must find space to offer my gratitude to the following, without whose help, enthusiasm, generosity and knowledge, this book would not have been so enriched: my friend and esteemed fellow crime historian, Stewart Evans and his good lady Rosie; James Nice; Alan and Joan Chapman; Robert 'Bookman' Wright; BBC Radio Norfolk; the late Syd Dernley; Jayne Whitwell; Brian Wild; John Forbes; Ken Jackson; Ray Noble; Peter Watson at *Family Tree* magazine; Clifford Elmer books; Les Bolland books; Philip Goodbody at Doormouse Bookshop; Brian Symonds at Burnham Market Pharmacy; Norfolk Probation Service; The Tolhouse Museum, Great Yarmouth; The Shirehall Museum and Bridewell at Walsingham; Wymondham Bridewell Museum; Norwich Castle Museum; Freda Wilkins-Jones and all the helpful staff at the Norfolk Record Office; University of East Anglia Library; the encyclopaedic knowledge of Michael Bean at Great Yarmouth library; Clive Wilkins-Jones and the superb staff at Norfolk Heritage Library; my friends amongst the past and present serving officers of Norfolk Constabulary; and of course, my old friends at the Norfolk Constabulary Archive.

Finally (but by no means least), I thank my family: especially my dear son Lawrence and my beloved Molly, for their love and support during the research of this book.

Note: all the photographs and illustrations are from the author's collection unless otherwise credited. All the modern photographs of murder sites, localities and gravestones have been specially taken by the author for this book in 2005 and 2006.

THE
LIFE and EXECUTION
OF
James Blomfield Rush,
For the MURDERS at Stanfield Hall, on the

Bodies of ISAAC JERMY and

JERMY JERMY, his son,

Who was Executed on the Castle Hill, on Saturday last, in April, 1849.

James Blomfield Rush, is the natural son of the daughter of a farmer, near Wymondham, by a farmer residing near the parish in or near which she lived, to whom she was engaged. From some cause the engagement was broken off, and an action was brought by her for breach of promise of marriage, and heavy damages obtained. Mr. Rush, of Aylsham, not long afterwards married the prisoner's mother. From this year until 1834, Rush's father occupied a farm at Felmingham, the property of the late Rev. George Preston, and subsequently of the late Mr. Jermy, where he died, his death having been attended by somewhat extraordinary circumstances. He was found dead in his kitchen in the day time, with a shot wound behind his ear, a discharged gun lying near him. Several reports were spread respecting this affair, and amongst them, one that a number of persons had been summoned to the house by the son, and when the Coroner arrived, he found his jury as it were ready to his hand. The verdict was Felo-de-se.

The prisoner was brought up by his mother's husband, and put to school with Mr. Nunn, at Eye, in Suffolk. In 1834 he commenced farming at Aylsham, under the Rev. Samuel Pitman, from whom he rented for about four years, 120 acres of land. In 1828 he married the second daughter of a highly respectable yeoman, in the neighbourhood of Aylsham, and took the Wood Dalling hall farm, under W. E. L. Bulwer, Esq. where he expended a considerable sum in improvements.

The husband of Rush's mother held a farm at Felmingham, under the Rev. George Preston. Times were very hard for farming, and he often talked of giving up his farms, and he said I should have what part I liked when he did so, but should prefer my taking the whole; in the mean time, one of his tenants at Felmingham would not hold under him any longer: he wished me to take that, he did so, under an agreement for 18 years, from Michaelmas, 1835, at £110 per annum.

He took the Stanfield hall farm for 21 years, at £500 per annum; In 1837 the Rev. George Preston died; Mr. Jermy, his son, the late Recorder, discovered the leases were not legally made, and this was the beginning of disputes between Mr. Rush and Mr. Jermy.

At the letter part of his occupation of Wood Dalling Hall Farm, Rush commenced and continued the business of valuer and auctioneer, in which he met with some success.

The Potash farm, which was the property of Mr. Calver, was for sale, and as it lies between the Stanfield Hall and Hethel properties of Mr. Jermy, that gentleman had a wish to possess it, as it would have made the property a compact whole. Rush consulted Mr. Jermy about its purchase, and the latter deputed him to buy it at a certain sum. However, the estate was run up to a higher sum than Mr. Jermy had directed Rush to bid, and Rush bought it for himself. The price was about 130l. above Mr. Jermy's bid. Rush informed Mr. Jermy, that although he (Rush) had purchased it, he did not possess the means to pay for it, and requested Mr. Jermy to pay for it, and requested Mr. Jermy to lend him the sum he required on mortgage, 3500l. was advanced for which interest was to be paid. After this two more sums were advanced, making 5000l. which was not to be called in until ten years after. This term expired two days after the murder.

The daughter of the prisoner, whose decease was confidently reported on saturday, had an interview with he father; she and the rest of the family are as well as under these melancholy circumstances can be expected. Miss Rush, and the younger branches of the family are still at Felmingham; with the exception of one son, who with his eldest brother, Mr. James Rush, is at Potash. The prisoner has nine children.

THE EXECUTION.

This morning the above unhappy culprit paid the forfeit of his life to the offended laws of his country. No execution of late years has attracted so large an assemblage of spectators, some thousands being present. About nine o'clock he took some refreshment, and shortly afterwards the sheriff arrived at the castle, and immediately proceeded to the condemned cell. The usual melancholy preparations having been completed, Rush was brought to the room where he was to be pinioned. He appeared to be quite calm and collected, and walked with a firm step. The melancholy procession then proceeded towards the scaffold, which he mounted without any assistance, and in less than a minute the drop fell, and the wretched malefactor was launched into eternity,

O Lord! receive my sinful soul, have mercy on my guilt;
The blood of Christ have made me whole, for me that blood was spilt!
All you that do around me stand, may this a warning be;
Unto the word of God attend, and shun bad company.
You see me here a wretched man, but short will be my stay;
Yet on my Saviour I'll depend, to wash my sins away.
Pray for my soul, good people all, and pity my sad fate;
A moment hence the drop will fall, I have not long to wait.
And may the blood of Jesus Christ, atonement for me make;
On his dear name my comfort rest, he died for sinners' sake.

WALKER, PRINTER, CHURCH STREET, ST. MILES, NORWICH.

A broadsheet sold at the execution of James Rush, 21 April 1849.

INTRODUCTION

Norfolk is one of England's five largest counties. An extensive outland of agrarian fields stretching from the eastern flank of Britain, almost half of the county is bounded by sea. Over much of the period covered by this book, Norfolk was not overpopulated, and many towns and village communities were still, by today's standards, insular and remote. The industrial towns of the North and 'big smoke' of London seemed a world away: their advanced transport systems, communications, density and diversity of human life sharply contrasting with the country ways of life. Back then, attitudes to life and death were very different. Families were larger, and it was a sad fact of life that due to epidemic diseases, bad sanitary provision and lack of affordable medical care, many did not make it to maturity. Widowhood and mourning black were the order of the day for numberless people for much of their lives.

Before the Temperance Movement took off in Norfolk, from about the 1880s, the local pub was the focal point of any village celebration, holiday or entertainment. Mind you, the path to temperance or 'blue ribboning' was not a smooth one: both men and women of the 'rough order' took exception to what they considered meddlesome interference by organisations like the Salvation Army (or as they called them, 'The Skeleton Army'), pelting them with whatever came to hand in the gutter as they paraded. Hence, the early bonnets worn by female Salvationists were more for protection than uniform appearance! In those days, men spent most of their spare time in pubs, perhaps taking part in pub sporting events such as skittles or quoits: but it still meant they were drinking. Indeed, a recurring theme in a number of Norfolk murder cases is the fact that the culprit was known to have been 'in drink', or even a habitual drunkard whose mind had become unhinged by alcohol abuse.

For most Norfolk people in the nineteenth and early twentieth centuries news was disseminated by word of mouth, newspapers and periodicals. In many areas country folk would eagerly await the arrival of the town and village carriers, bringing the latest news from the big towns and the city. As ever, a local murder always attracted a premium of interest: from the horror of its discovery, through the tracking of the murderer, and on to the trial – people often forming their own opinions for or against the accused. If the case had gained some notoriety the papers would be filled with columns detailing every aspect of the case, and many would eagerly watch for the jury's verdict: for if it was 'Guilty' they could be in for what they considered a treat! Before the public execution of felons was banned by parliament in 1868 and removed out of sight behind prison walls – in the days before professional football matches, film shows and television – a hanging was a real 'event'. Thousands of men, women and children – numbers equalling that of football match capacity crowds – would fill the open ground and cram into the windows of nearby houses to watch the proceedings. Many would have set out in the wee hours of the morning, walking miles to guarantee themselves a good view of the execution.

Most executions in Norfolk were carried out in front of the old County Gaol at Norwich Castle, between the two small gatehouses at the foot of the entrance slope. Crowds would spread across the horse and cattle market, temporary wooden stands would be built to enable grandstand views, while the gentry paid handsomely for private rooms in buildings overlooking the scaffold. As the crowds gathered, 'long song sellers' sold broadsheets recounting the story of the murder and probably the criminal's condemned cell confession in words, pictures and poetry. Gin and tea wagons sold brews by the cup, while hawkers of hot pies, potatoes, pastries and fancies did a good trade – as did the pickpockets, who regularly managed quite a haul of purses and watches at such events.

As the appointed hour approached, the great bell of St Peter Mancroft church would toll away the final minutes. Then an entourage of civic dignitaries with attendant javelin men and prison officials filed out from the prison gates, followed by the Prison Chaplain and the condemned felon, flanked by Governor and warders. It was quite a spectacle. Upon arrival at the scaffold an expectant hush would fall over the crowd, and as the condemned man or woman mounted the steps of the gallows, cries of 'Hats off!' came from the crowd. This was not a mark of respect, but a desire for a better view from those at the back. With an adjustment of the rope, and the pulling down of a white hood, the executioner – the 'Lord of the Scaffold' – would push the lever, release the trapdoor, and the condemned would be plunged to eternity. Connoisseurs among the crowd noted the efficiency of the executioner by the speed with which signs of life departed from his victim.

If the executioner thought the drop had not gone well he would nip down below the scaffold and pull on the legs of the person being 'swung', to hasten them on their way. The body would then be left to hang for the appointed hour, to ensure all life was extinct, and as a grim warning for all to see. The body would then be taken down and the crowd would depart. But, in the days when the bodies of executed criminals were passed to surgeons for dissection, a few hardy souls would have lingered to view the body in the 'Surgeon's Hall', after the initial cuts had been rendered. And even in the years after dissection of executed felons had ceased, it was not unknown for the prisoners of the County Gaol to be paraded in the exercise yard as the corpse was wheeled through in an open 'shell' coffin for all to see. Even up to the last days of hanging, it was customary for the bodies of those who had been executed to be buried and covered with quicklime (to hasten decomposition) within the precincts of the prison where they had been hanged. The initials of the executed person and the year of their execution, carved into a white stone let into the wall nearby, was the only grave marker allowed.

The Victorians, so proud and willing to extol the virtues of morality and 'sensibilities', were satisfied with the removal of the 'animal spectacle' of public executions to within the prison walls: out of sight, out of mind . . . or was it? The hypocrisy of the situation is revealed when sales of righteous publications and religious journals, such as *Home Words* or *The Quiver* (said to be 'worthy of a place in every home'), were being eclipsed by lurid products of the gutter press, like the infamous *Illustrated Police News* and the equally graphic *Penny Illustrated Paper*. Furthermore, publications such as the *Famous Crimes Series*, edited by Harold Furniss, were enjoyed well into the late Edwardian period. Thus, removal of the spectacle of public execution only seemed to fuel a morbid interest in it, adding to the mystique and fascination of the dark netherworld of crime and criminals – and especially murderers.

In this book it is my privilege and pleasure to share with the reader many previously unpublished, or long unseen, accounts and photographs, relating to some of the most infamous, intriguing and notable crimes ever committed in the fair county of Norfolk. In the course of research I have visited most of the sites involved, actually standing on spots where several of the murders took place. My investigations have even led me to visit some of the prisons and bridewells where the perpetrators were held. For instance, accompanied by a party of my WEA students, I visited the remarkable and unspoilt Walsingham Bridewell, where Fanny Billing and Cat Frary (her name is also spelt as Frarey in some accounts) were interrogated and held for months pending trial. The atmosphere lingering in its dark corridors and tragic cells was so intense, so oppressive and sad, that some of my students were unable to remain inside and immediately walked out. Today, some of the sites have been altered beyond recall or demolished, like James Rush's home, Potash Farm, or the cottages where the Burnham poisoners lived. Most of the sites look innocent enough now, cluttered with housing and business developments, with motor cars roaring past: yet a shudder can still run down your spine when you consider what happened there. Standing by the graves of some of the victims, especially having studied their cases, one feels moved by the simple stones, which often give little clue to the story behind them.

I have had a chance to see for myself original letters written in the hand of some of the criminals featured in these stories, the same hands that committed the most abominable of deeds. From America I obtained a copy of *The Trial of James Blomfield Rush* with annotations by a member of the prosecuting counsel. I have even held the full head and neck death mask of Rush, a cast

The Judge leaving Norwich Cathedral after the Assize service, *c*. 1912.

that, chillingly, still clearly evinced the deep ridge forged into his neck by the rope that hanged him. To me, the most fascinating of all paperwork was to find the death warrant for the execution of Robert Goodale – one of the most infamous executions of all time – in the Norfolk Records Office. I have touched some of the relics of the crimes: most movingly, the mangled collar numbers blasted from the uniform of PC Alger by a mentally unstable ne'er-do-well wielding a shotgun. And finally, having rediscovered Norfolk's all-but-forgotten cause célèbre of the Edwardian period, I have managed to track down an original photograph of the woman at the centre of it all – Rosa Kowen.

In recounting these ten cases I hope I can convey some of the lasting impressions from my research. To this end, I have attempted to recreate the atmosphere of past times and past crimes by evoking the language and details of contemporary accounts. These I have carefully blended with as much original source material, witness statements, coroners' reports and original court records as possible, in an attempt to strip away the myths that have become attached to these crimes over the years. Indeed, it proved to be the case that each original, unvarnished tale required no embroidery to amaze and appal. In fact, these stories – with their memorable characters and their intriguing twists and turns – have proved, yet again, Byron's adage: 'Truth is strange, stranger than fiction.'

Neil R. Storey
Norfolk 2006

1

THE BURNHAM SICKNESS

Burnham 1835

The seven Burnhams are villages dotted along the upper edge of the Norfolk coast. These attractive settlements are blessed with a combination of big skies, fine countryside, and rivers that snake towards quiet bays and the sea. Today they are beloved by holidaymakers and second homeowners, but in the nineteenth century they were rural hamlets of close-knit communities with a strong reliance on agriculture, coastal trading, and a long history of smuggling. In 1835 Burnham Market and its adjoining hamlet of Burnham Westgate was a community of 1,126 inhabitants. Life was simple and there were still many who not only believed in, but relied on, folklore to ensure good harvests, administer medical needs, and even find love. Death was common: parents accepted that not all of their children would make it to maturity, and consequently, families were larger than they are today. And in Victorian times there was always a fear of epidemics and diseases, especially smallpox, consumption (tuberculosis) and cholera.

Folks here lived close by one another, many of them in small rows of cottage homes, which often had shared yards, pumps, adjoining workshops and stables. On one of these roads, known today as North Street, just off Burnham's marketplace, lived the Billing, Frary and Taylor families. Their row of cottages led off from the street at a right angle. Nearest the road, living in the cramped rooms above Thomas Lake's carpenter's shop, were Robert and Catherine Frary with their three children. Next to them were Peter and Mary Taylor, and finally, on this little row, lived James and Frances 'Fanny' Billing with a number of their children.

Two sudden deaths occurred in quick succession within the Frary household early in March 1835, leaving poor Cat Frary (aged forty) mourning for the loss of her husband and a child who had been staying with her. There was public sympathy for her, but inevitable questions were raised in fear of some contagion having manifested itself in the Frary home. Time passed, however, and as no one else showed signs of falling victim to the mysterious 'Burnham Sickness', the matter died down and the village returned to normal for a few weeks. But then Mary Taylor (wife of Peter Taylor, aged forty-five, a journeyman cobbler who was a neighbour and friend of the Frarys) was taken violently ill and dropped dead on the evening of 12 March. Mr Cremer, the local surgeon had been summoned by Cat Frary and Phoebe Taylor (Mary's sister-in-law) but could do nothing for poor Mary. Surgeon Cremer's suspicions were aroused by this sudden death and an inquest was called for the following day, before Mr F.T. Quarles, Coroner for the Duchy of Lancaster. At the inquest it was suggested that Peter Taylor had been 'associated' with Fanny Billing (aged forty-six), a mother of eight children (she had given birth to a total of eleven children but three had died in infancy), who was described as 'a woman of loose character', but this dalliance was not immediately considered relevant to the crime. The contents of Mary Taylor's stomach had been analysed and found to contain arsenic in such a quantity it had caused her death. The jury returned a verdict of death by poisoning: but exactly how, and by whose hand, remained unknown. But the groundswell of suspicion within Burnham fell on Mary's slothful and unfaithful husband, Peter Taylor.

Further enquiries soon revealed that Fanny Billing had recently bought arsenic from the local chemist, Henry Nash. When questioned about this, Billing claimed she was buying it to poison rats and mice for a Mrs Webster of Creake – a statement Mrs Webster flatly denied. A poke (small sack) of

The marketplace, Burnham in 1900 had changed little since 1835.

flour from the Taylor house had been tested and traces of arsenic were found: this was enough for local magistrates Frederick Hare and Henry Blyth to remand Peter Taylor and Fanny Billing to Walsingham Bridewell for further questioning.

As Billing was escorted by constables to the cart that would take her to the bridewell, Frary was quoted as calling out: 'Mor, hold your own and they cannot hurt us.' This outburst was quoted in early accounts as being the cause of Frary's immediate arrest, but that was not quite the case. Rather than relying on the spurious claim that Frary made that statement, further investigations led to more solid grounds for her arrest in connection with the murder. Both Cat and Fanny were known to consult witches or 'cunning folk' at Burnham, Sall and Wells. On the afternoon of Fanny's arrest Cat asked Fanny's son, Joseph, to hire her a horse and gig for a drive to Sall, in order to see a woman who – as Joseph recalled – 'was something of a witch, that that woman might tie Mr Curtis's tongue [Mr Curtis was the keeper of the Walsingham Bridewell] so that he might not question my mother.' Frary's close friendship with Billing, combined with their trips to the witches and the poisoning of Mary Taylor, revived the questions that still surrounded the mysterious death of Frary's husband and the child staying with them. These factors led to Cat Frary being taken into custody for questioning.

As the weight of evidence against her was revealed through questioning, Cat Frary – who had appeared so 'cock sure' – soon buckled under the pressure and went into rapid physical and mental decline. Needless to say, the alchemy of the witches did nothing to hold the tongue of Mr Curtis. Worse still, comparisons were drawn with a woman named Mary Wright, from the nearby village of Wighton, who had murdered her husband by administering arsenic only a few months before the Burnham deaths: and Mary Wright, Billing and Frary were known to have consulted the same 'cunning woman' or 'witch' – Hannah Shorten of Wells. Shorten's 'love-spells' were known to consist of arsenic and salt mixed together and then thrown on the fire. For most Burnham people, it did not require a great leap of imagination to see the likes of the accused mix the poisonous concoction in the food of one who would have obstructed their 'sinful desires'.

By the time of the Summer Assizes the bill against Peter Taylor had been ignored by the Grand Jury. Concerns over Frary's deteriorating health raised questions of her ability to stand trial, but nonetheless, Billing and Frary appeared in the dock before Mr Baron Bolland on Friday 7 August 1835. Investigations had concluded that the women had entered into a diabolical plot to bring about the removal of each other's 'human obstacles' – quid pro quo. Frary was charged with administering poison to Mary Taylor, with Billing as an accessory before the fact. The second indictment charged them both with murdering Robert Frary. The death of the child was not mentioned in the charges.

The corridor of Walsingham Bridewell, where Billing and Frary were interrogated and detained to await their appearance at the Assizes. The spirit and health of Catherine Frary were so broken within these walls that concerns were raised about her ability to stand trial.

Phoebe Taylor was the first to take the stand. She recalled visiting her brother-in-law, Peter Taylor, at his house on the evening of Mary Taylor's death. When Phoebe arrived about 8pm she went upstairs to find Mary on a chair at the bedside, retching. Asked how she was, Mary said she felt 'very ill', adding that Mrs Frary was boiling gruel for her. Mary then asked Phoebe to go and fetch the gruel for her. When she arrived at Cat Frary's, Phoebe saw a saucepan by the side of the fire. Cat poured a little gruel into a cup and Phoebe took it to Mary, who, after having it thinned a little, partook of it. Mary's sickness had not improved when Phoebe returned about 12.20am. By that time Mary was so weak she could not speak: Peter Taylor was also retching. Peter sent Frary to summon Surgeon Cremer and Phoebe was sent to go with her. When Mr Cremer arrived there was nothing he could do for Mary Taylor and she died shortly afterwards.

Phoebe Taylor's story was corroborated by two other visitors to the Taylor house on that fateful night – a local labourer named Edward Sparke and blacksmith William Powell, who had come to see Peter Taylor for a haircut and shave. Both men stated they had seen Frary taking additional cups of gruel to Mrs Taylor; and noted that after she poured the gruel into the teacup, she openly 'took a small paper out of her pocket, and emptied the contents into the gruel and stirred it up'. Sparke noted the contents were white, like powdered lump sugar – indeed, that is what he assumed the contents of the packet were. Frary was then seen to throw the empty white paper onto the fire. The evidence became yet more damning with the testimony of Samuel Fuller Salmon, an employee of Henry Nash the chemist. He recalled the visit of Fanny Billing and Cat Frary to the chemist shop on 25 February. Mrs Frary had asked for a pennyworth of arsenic, claiming it was 'to poison mice with'. Billing also requested a pennyworth and Salmon wrapped both pennyworths (which equated to a quarter of an ounce) of white arsenic in separate white papers, gumming a label marked 'Poison' on each.

The chemist Henry Nash also gave evidence. He recalled a subsequent visit, when Fanny Billing came to the shop with Jane Dixon (it must be remembered that, in those days, a witness had to be present if poisons were to be purchased). Billing asked for three-pennyworth of arsenic, claiming she was buying it at the behest of Mrs Webster of Creake, to kill her infestation of mice and rats. Nash recalled she then asked for a pennyworth more for

herself, plus a pennyworth of pills and a pennyworth of lemon drops: all of which – he took pains to point out to the court – were put into separate packets and the poisons clearly marked. Jane Dixon was paid a penny by Frary for her trouble.

Francis Church, the Burnham Westgate surgeon had been directed by the Coroner to make an examination of the body of Mary Taylor. In the company of Surgeon Albert Cremer he had gone to the Taylor house, opened Mary's body, and found 'an appearance of inflammation on the external coat and on a portion of the bowels'. He removed the stomach, being careful to pass a ligature at each end. Church placed

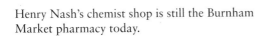

Henry Nash's chemist shop is still the Burnham Market pharmacy today.

the stomach in a bowl and Cremer had the dubious honour of carrying it over with Mr Church to Nash's chemist shop. In the presence of all these medical men, tests were carried out by Nash on the stomach contents and arsenic was detected. A portion of this stomach was also sent to Richard Griffin, a Norwich surgeon. His tests also revealed the presence of arsenic. The results of tests, which revealed arsenic from flour in the Taylor residence, were also presented.

The method of the murder and the possession of poison by Billing and Frary established, the court was then presented with the motive for the death

3 Dreadful Murders
BY POISON.

A full and true account of the dreadful and shocking Murder committed last week at BURNHAM MARKET, in the County of Norfolk on Mary, the wife of PETER TAYLOR, a journeyman shoemaker of that place; showing how she met with a painful but very sudden death by ARSENIC BEING MIXED WITH HER FOOD, as is suspected by her husband and two women of loose character with whom he was connected; and containing also a further account of the death of Mr. FRARY and a child who died in the same place as is suspected by the same treacherous means.

Some of the most distressing and harrowing murders ever remembered in the County of Norfolk, not even excepting the case of MARY WRIGHT, have just been perpetrated at Burnham Market, and have produced a surprising degree of excitement in that town and neighbourhood. On Thursday morning the 12th day of the present month, MARY TAYLOR, a married woman between 40 and 50 years of age, was taken very ill, and on Mr. Cremer the the surgeon being sent for he at once saw and said she was poisoned; and although all was done that could be done to save her life the poor women died the same night in the greatest agony. An Inquest was held on the following day before F. T. Quarles, Gent. Coroner for the Duchy of Lancaster; but there being then no proof of how the deceased came by the poison, although it was evident that her death had been caused by taking it, the Jury found a verdict to the effect that she died from the effects of arsenic, but by what means administered was unknown. It being remembered, however, in the neighbourhood, that there had been an intimacy between the husband of the deceased and Fanny Billing, a married woman living at the next door, and she being of a loose character, other inquiries were made It was then found that this Fanny Billing had a short time previous purchased some arsenic of a neighbouring druggist, saying at the time that she wanted it for a Mrs. Webster of Creake to poison some vermin with it. These rumours increased so much that two Magistrates in the neighbourhood (Frederick Hare and Henry Blyth, Esqrs.) thought proper to hold a special Meeting at the Hoste Arms, on the following Wednesday and summon the parties concerned before them. Mrs. Webster of Creake, denied ever having employed Billing to purchase poison;—a quantity of arsenic was found in Taylor's house mixed with some flour in a poke from which the deceased had

eaten, and it seemed surprising that if the husband knew nothing of, he should not be poisoned too, but he, it seems, was not effected. Taylor and Billing were at once taken into close custody, and several examinations have succeeded, which have caused, we understand, their being both fully committed to Walsingham Bridewell to take their trials for the murder next week at the assizes. As Billing was about to be removed by the Constables, a woman by the name of Frary, who had also been living near them, was over-heard to say to her " Mor hold your own, and they cannot hurt us." This led to other suspicions, especially as Frary's husband, and a child which had lived with them, had died 2 or three weeks before very suddenly. Frary was then also taken into custody, & the bodies of the husband and child disinterred & examined as to whether they died by poison. Their stomachs were brought to Norwich to be analized, and although we have not yet learned the result there is hardly any doubt but that their lives were taken by the same treacherous means. Taylor, whose family we believe live at Whissonset, has been married near 20 years, and although there is no family, always appeared to live very comfortably with his wife: he has, too, always borne a steady moral character, and was a singer in the Dissenters' Meeting House in that Town for many years. The wife was a most steady and industrious woman, frequently maintaining both her husband, and herself by her industry he being frequently incapable of working from ill health, and this she has done entirely since last Whitsuntide.

Well might SOLOMON say of a loose woman—" he that goeth after her is as an Ox going to the slaughter, or a fool to the correction of the stocks: he goeth after her straitway 'til a dart strike through his liver,— as a bird hasteth to the snare, and knoweth not that it is for his life."

[WALKER, PRINTER, ORFORD-HILL.]

A contemporary broadsheet relating the case of the Burnham poisoners.

of Mary Taylor. At the inquest and previous hearing, allusions had been made about illicit liaisons between Billing and Taylor. At the trial the court was presented with the testimony of several locals willing to state the affair between Billing and Taylor had been public knowledge, and that the couple had been spotted together on several occasions, loitering in the shadows by the Rose and Crown, and in the lovers' lanes around the village. More than once, it was stated, Peter Taylor had been 'obliged to take the hedges, leap gates and run across fields' to avoid detection. Such was the feeling of dislike in the village for Taylor's indiscreet behaviour, he found his shoemaking trade had tailed off, and in the last few months of his life Mary was more or less keeping him. Taylor claimed he was suffering from rheumatic fever and confined to his bed: but it was remarked in court how he miraculously recovered enough in the evenings to conduct his liaisons with Billing and evade prying eyes by running across fields. The court was also reminded of the time James Billing had been brought before the Walsingham Petty Sessions, where he was charged with 'ill-using' Fanny. In claiming extenuating circumstances he cited his behaviour had been a direct result of discovering his wife and Peter Taylor in the privy together. Apparently it had been the last straw after he had, on a prior occasion, tried to enter his living room and found the door bolted. When he was finally allowed in, he had found the pair alone in there! Even Fanny Billing's son testified he had remonstrated with his mother about her relationship with Taylor. She had promised to break it off: that same week Mrs Taylor died.

When Cat Frary took the stand her relationship with a Mr Gridley came under scrutiny. Billing testified that together they, Billing and Frary, had bought arsenic to cast a 'love-spell' as told to them by the 'witch', Mother Shorten of Wells. Frary had said: 'I am going to put a handful of salt and a teaspoonful of arsenic into the fire of a morning to draw Mr Gridley to see me again at night.'

It was claimed she had met Gridley on ten occasions. One night she was caught out by her husband, who demanded to know her business with the man. When Gridley found out about the exchange, Billing stated he had said of Mr Frary: 'Damn him, put him out of the way, he is of no use here!' A few days later Cat Frary went to Billing and asked her to put some of the love philtre (potion) into a small bottle of porter. This just made the poor man sick. The following day Billing and Frary conspired to get more arsenic and mixed it with the gruel, tea and brandy she gave her husband. His death was excruciating. In her testimony Billing claimed: 'I was present when he died; I went upstairs after his death, and after the people's backs were turned a little from her, she [Frary] clapped her hands and said "I am glad he's dead."' Billing went on to point out that it was Frary who had put the 'stuff' in the flour.

When Billing encountered Frary on the afternoon of Mary Taylor's death she asked how the woman was. Frary clapped her hands and said: 'I have stretched her out.' After Mary's death Frary gave Billing some flour in a bag and some bran in a cloth from the Taylors' house, telling her to put it in her swill tub. Frary also said she had put the remainder of the dumpling from the Taylors' into the privy. Frary was either too ill or chose not to speak against Billing's statement. On being called for their defence both women declared their innocence, but declined to say anything further, saying they should leave it to their counsel. They called no witnesses. After a brief summing-up the Judge allowed the jury to retire to deliberate their verdict. Billing and Frary were both found guilty as charged.

The second indictment charged Billing and Frary with the murder of Robert Frary. Elizabeth Southgate, the mother of the child that died while staying at the Frarys', gave evidence of visiting the household the day after her child's death to enquire after the circumstances. She found Robert Frary very ill. While she was there Fanny Billing came in with some porter. Asking Cat for a teacup, Fanny was seen to swill the porter around in the jug before she poured it out in the cup. Southgate noted: 'Something came out of the spout like powdered lump sugar not dissolved.' Billing then passed it to Frary, saying: 'Drink it all up Mr Frary, it will do you good.' When he did not drink it down she urged him again: 'Drink it up.' Bob Frary retched for most of the afternoon and by seven the following morning he could not speak. By 8am he was dead. Assumed to have fallen victim to some mystery illness, he was buried a few days later.

After Mary Taylor's death was confirmed as a murderous poisoning, the question of the deaths in the Frary household flared up again, and the body of Robert Frary was exhumed. A curious feature of death by arsenic poisoning is that it can result in the corpse being 'preserved' – putrefaction taking longer due to the nature of the poison in the system. Robert Frary had been buried for three weeks. Surgeon Church, who examined the body stated in cross-examination: 'The body was as fresh as if buried but a day.' When examined, the stomach still showed inflammation, and when tested it clearly indicated a fatal amount of arsenic. The prisoners, again, said nothing in their defence, nor called any witnesses. After a short deliberation the jury found both women guilty.

The learned Judge was observed as being 'deeply affected' while donning the black cap to pass sentence. As he addressed the condemned women, Billing appeared to be 'earnestly praying'. Frary, near collapse, had to be held up, and through her trembling lips passed the words: 'I am not guilty, my Lord.' Once sentence was pronounced Frary had to be removed from the bar in hysterics, and 'bitter shrieks' – supposed to come from the families of the condemned women – were heard from the overflowing public gallery.

Frances Billing and Catherine Frary dictated their confessions to the murders in their condemned cells. They admitted their crimes, adding that they had not only mixed arsenic with Mr Frary's porter and gruel, but with

Burnham Westgate church and graveyard from which the body of Robert Frary was exhumed.

his pills, and that it took no fewer than four doses of the poison in the poor man's porter and tea to kill him. They were executed in front of the County Gaol at Norwich Castle on Monday 10 August 1835. The scaffold was usually assembled between the entrance lodges, but 'out of proper consideration for the exhausted condemned, whose bodily powers would prove inadequate to sustain them in walking the distance' the scaffold was erected at the upper end of the bridge. This also made the proceedings visible to most of the vast crowd assembled to watch the final moments of the two women, shamed in the press and broadsheets as 'The Burnham Poisoners'. It was commented that the crowd, which numbered several thousand, was seen to be made up of an extraordinary number of women.

Shortly before the hour of twelve the executioner suspended two ropes from the gallows beam. As the clocks of the city struck noon the great gates of the prison opened. The officers of justice – Under-Sheriff, Gaoler, entourage and javelin men – walked out smartly. The Chaplain, Revd James Brown, followed a little behind, walking slowly, and reading the burial service aloud. Behind him walked the two condemned women. Frary was dressed in widow's weeds. Billing wore her 'coloured clothes'. Both had handkerchiefs covering their faces and were supported by two prison wardresses each. Billing walked with what appeared to be a firm step; Frary was near collapse and had to be carried up the steps of the scaffold. Placed on the gallows trapdoor, and the ropes put around their necks, the women held hands. The fatal bolt was drawn, the trap fell open, and the women were plunged into eternity. Billing died with scarcely a struggle; Frary was much convulsed for several seconds. The silence that had hitherto pervaded was broken by a piercing shriek when the drop fell. Then all was still again, and the crowd of observers began drifting away.

The illustrated broadsheet and long song sellers saw a roaring trade on that day. Even the sermon preached by the Revd John Spurgin on the Sunday after the execution, in the parish church of Docking, was printed, published and sold in hundreds, at 4d each or 3s 6d a dozen for distribution!

Peter Taylor remained in Norwich after the trial and even went to see the execution. When eyes had fallen away from the main spectacle, the many people who had travelled from Burnham to watch the event recognised Taylor and felt aggrieved at his tenacity in coming to witness the demise of Cat and Fanny. Many felt he was equally complicit in the crimes and it was only through the early intervention of his friends that Taylor beat a hasty retreat from the crowd. Taylor attempted to return to his brother's house but the people of Burnham wanted him out of the village. A mob of villagers attacked the house, smashing windows and breaking down the doors. Gaining entry, they demanded that Taylor be handed over to them. They were told he was not there. He was, in fact, hidden in the closet. When the mob had left, Taylor fled to his father's house, only to be rearrested on new evidence coming to light, which revealed him to be more involved with the murders than previously believed. Brought before the magistrates he was recommitted for trial at the Assizes. In all, Taylor would serve twelve months in prison before eventually standing trial.

The trial opened on 1 April at the 1836 Spring Assizes, and was conducted before Mr Justice Gaselee. The new evidence came from witnesses who had been questioned directly about Billing and Frary. The witnesses were at pains to point out that if the earlier questioning had been directly related to Peter Taylor, they would have offered their evidence earlier. The two key witnesses were Elizabeth Southgate and Edward Sparke. Southgate, while visiting Cat Frary on the morning before Mary Taylor died, had observed Fanny Billing and Peter Taylor going into the privy together. Five minutes later they came out and she saw Billing pass Taylor a small paper packet, saying, 'Here is enough for her.'

Edward Sparke also testified that when he visited the Frarys' house on that fateful day, he observed Mrs Billing get up, go to the window, and putting her arm out, make a signal before going downstairs. Standing against the window, he observed Billing and Taylor meeting in the yard below at the corner of Lake's shop. Sparke went on to state he overheard a conversation when they were parting: Taylor clapped his hand on Billing's shoulder and said: 'Never

A broadsheet sold at the execution of Billing and Frary, the last time a double execution of women was carried out in Norfolk, 10 August 1835.

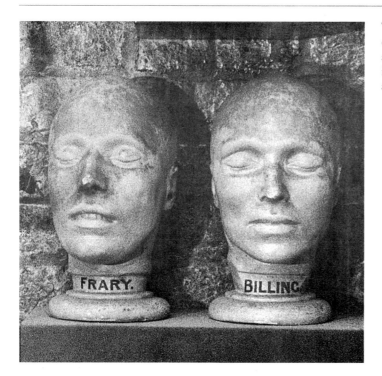

The death masks of Catherine Frary and Frances Billing in their old display at Norwich Castle.

mind, she will soon be done away with, and it will soon be all right with us.' Sparke also reiterated his statement from the previous trial, detailing how he saw Cat Frary administer the powder from a packet in her pocket into the gruel for Mrs Taylor.

Then James Billing took the stand and recounted how he had discovered his wife's infidelity with neighbour Peter Taylor. It amounted to a sorry tale, and despite brave attempts by the defence counsel to score a few points against the character and credibility of the witnesses, the jury were convinced of Taylor's guilt and passed verdict accordingly. Thus Peter Taylor was sentenced to death – the trial had lasted eleven hours.

No confession emanated from the condemned cell. His execution was set for noon on 23 April 1836 and Peter Taylor swore his innocence to the end. The scaffold was situated in front of the castle, as it had been for Fanny and Cat. Thousands came to see the denouement of the sordid triangle of the Burnham poisoners. Taylor, like Cat, had to be supported and almost carried to the scaffold trap. A contemporary account states:

He appeared to be shabbily dressed, and struggled but slightly after being turned off . . . scarcely an expression of pity for the malefactor was heard from any one, though very unusual on these occasions; but all appeared to concur in the opinion, that he richly merited the punishment he was condemned to undergo.

2

THE STANFIELD HALL MURDER

Wymondham 1848

It was one of the most infamous crimes of the nineteenth century. Books and broadsheets recounting every lurid detail of the murder sold in un-precedented numbers: the broadsheet of the murderer's 'Sorrowful Lamentations' sold an incredible 2½ million copies across the country; columns, pages and whole supplements were given over to it in both local and national papers. Queen Victoria is known to have taken a personal interest in the case, and Charles Dickens – perhaps the greatest author of his day – visited the scene, recording that it had: 'a murderous look that seemed to invite such a crime.' Simply the name of this location stimulated talk of the dastardly deeds connected with it. And the name was Stanfield Hall.

James Blomfield Rush (Blomfield was also recorded at the time as Blomefield and Bloomfield), the perpetrator of the murders, fitted the bill of a classic Victorian melodrama villain: not only in physical appearance, but in behaviour, manners and morals. His wax image – 'taken from life at Norwich' – was undoubtedly the star attraction in Madame Tussaud's Chamber of Horrors in the last year of the great lady's life. Visitors were recorded as looking into his cold, glassy eyes 'with the most painful interest'. The notoriety of James Blomfield Rush ensured his figure was on display in the Chamber for over 120 years.

Rush was not born into a criminal family or background – although he was born to Mary Blomfield out of wedlock, at a time when scorn was poured on illegitimacy. Rush was baptised in Tacolneston church on 10 January 1800. His father, William Howe, was successfully sued for breach of promise to Mary, who was awarded damages enough to provide a good dowry for her second marriage to Old Buckenham farmer John Rush in 1802. John Rush seems to have taken to young James. He permitted him to assume the name of Rush, and procured for him a good education at the grammar school of Mr Nunn, at Eye in Suffolk. Young James Rush took on his first farm as a tenant in 1824. Situated near Aylsham, this farm yielded well, and James became a good prospect for the young women of Aylsham. In the event, he married

Susannah Soames, a member of a well-known local family in May 1828. In that same year, James Rush took on another farm at Wood Dalling. Over the next twelve years James and Susannah were blessed with nine children that survived infancy.

In the publications written with hindsight after his execution, Rush was condemned as 'always a bad one' – a debauched deceiver and swindler. Some even went so far as to record they 'had always said Rush will be hanged'. Rush, who was always known for living beyond his means, took his first step on the road of deceit and crime while at Wood Dalling. Perhaps it was an unfortunate accident that one of his haystacks caught fire: but Rush was accused of arson, narrowly missing being put on trial. His insurance company initially refused to cough up for the loss of the haystack, but eventually agreed to pay out a reduced compensation.

Rush's reputation was not helped when it became known he had studied books by authors who had inspired revolution in America and France. Rush had read William Cobbett and Thomas Paine's *Age of Reason*. It was claimed Rush 'drank in the draughts of poison it contained, their pernicious influence became visible in his whole demeanour.' His Republican opinions were well known and he joined the infamous Revolution Club in Norwich. Rush kept company 'with some of the most violent and low artisans' in the city, visiting

Stanfield Hall from a contemporary engraving.

James Rush, drawn from life, in the dock at the Shirehall.

the pubs and clubs frequented by such men. At one of these clubs Rush shared membership with Richard Nockolds, one of the militant activists during the Norwich weaving riots of 1830. Nockolds confessed to throwing sulphuric acid in the face of John Wright, one of the master manufacturers during the dispute. Nockolds was eventually executed on Saturday 9 April 1831 for arson – specifically, firing haystacks and barns at Swanton Abbott. And during the machine breaking riots of 1830, when some of the rioters who had wrecked machines at Foulsham escaped across Rush's land, he personally helped them evade capture. For this Rush was brought before the Spring Assizes at Thetford in March 1831: he was lucky to get away with being bound over to keep the peace.

In 1835 James Rush rented a farm at Felmingham, right next to the one his father had taken on in 1811. They both shared the same landlord, Revd George Preston, Rector of Beeston St Lawrence and the 'owner' of Stanfield Hall. Preston trusted Rush, and as the Reverend's age and infirmity increased, he placed more and more confidence in him: appointing him his estate agent, steward and bailiff. In 1837 the elderly Revd Preston died and his eldest son, Isaac, inherited Stanfield Hall. A well-versed and successful lawyer, Isaac Preston had been made Recorder of Norwich in 1831. In order to 'regularise' his ownership of the Stanfield Hall Estate, Isaac Preston applied for, and was granted, the right to assume the surname and arms of Jermy – the old family connected to the Hall and distant relations of the Prestons. Rush continued to assist in the running of the farms and estates, although it must be said his relationship with the astute Isaac was never as close as that with his indulgent father.

The will of Revd Preston was not enacted without challenge. Thomas Jermy, a member of another branch of the family, and his cousin John Larner both believed they had claims on the Hall and estate. Their legal machinations gathered pace and matters soon turned nasty. In June 1838 Isaac Jermy put some of Revd Preston's effects up for auction, but was immediately served with notices to stop the sale by Thomas Jermy and John Larner. Larner then made an attempt to seize the Hall but was thrown out by Rush, acting as Bailiff for Jermy. Notices warning local labourers not to work for Isaac Jermy – lest they face legal action from the 'rightful Heir at Law' – were circulated in the district. Matters came to a violent head on 24 September when Larner and a band of about eighty men, recruited from local labouring stock, marched on Stanfield Hall and stormed the house. Isaac Jermy read the Riot Act, local constables were overpowered, and it was only with the arrival of the magistrates and the 4th Dragoon Guards, summoned from Norwich, that order was restored. The troops were instructed to prime their muskets and load with ball cartridge, and the besiegers were called on to surrender, which they did, before being carted away to imprisonment, pending an appearance at the Lent Assizes.

Despite their gallant defence of the hall, the relationship between Isaac Jermy and James Rush was ambiguous. Perhaps both men were always looking for angles and legal loopholes to widen their business interests and increase their wealth: some deals they transacted with each other were amicable, but some were 'a little sharp'. Isaac Jermy had empowered Rush to buy Potash Farm, adjoining Stanfield Hall, in 1838, but he instructed Rush not to exceed £3,500 in his bid. Rush, however, purchased it for himself for £3,750. This was to backfire on Rush. As he did not have the money to pay for the farm, he induced Isaac to advance it to him in the form of a mortgage. Jermy was shrewd; he knew Rush was bad with money, so under the terms of the mortgage Rush, in effect, became Jermy's tenant at Potash Farm. In this way, Jermy held the power to seize or confiscate the property if – or perhaps more likely when – Rush fell behind with his repayments, including the interest on the loan. The money thus secured was to remain on loan until 30 November 1848.

Rush's money troubles were compounded when Jermy found the leases on the Rush farms at Felmingham had been improperly drawn up and were not binding. Isaac had them redrawn and increased the rents. Arguably, this act was the first spark that set Rush ablaze with hatred for Jermy. These increased rents, plus the mortgage on Potash Farm, put Rush further and further in Jermy's debt.

Rush brushed with the law again in 1839, in an action reminiscent of that taken by his mother against his father. He was brought before the court by Miss Dank for breach of promise of marriage and seduction, the plaintiff having been reduced to seeking shelter in the workhouse after Rush turned his back on her. Rush lost the case and was ordered to pay damages.

By 1843 Rush was heavily indebted and his wife died 'after a lingering illness' at their farm in Felmingham. During her confinement to bed it was noted Rush was 'very attentive'. Maybe we should not be sceptical about his motives or suspect any foul play that may have speeded her demise? Certainly,

Potash Farm (now demolished), *c.* 1905.

James did not benefit from his wife's will, as she placed everything in trust for the benefit of her children. But then Rush forged a codicil that placed the property in his power until his youngest child reached the age of twenty-one.

In October 1844 another family tragedy occurred. James's stepfather John was found dead in his kitchen from a shotgun wound. James had been over on a visit and they had been shooting together. James stated his father had admired his gun, and he had left him poring over it in the kitchen, while he went upstairs to wash. James claimed he heard the gunshot, dashed back into the kitchen, and found 'to his horror, the gun had gone off'. Entering through the left cheek, the entire contents of the blast had lodged in his father's head, killing him instantly. There were grave doubts that Mr Rush Snr could have inflicted the fatal wound on himself. Nevertheless, the inquest recorded a verdict of 'Accidental death'. John Rush left an estate worth over £7,000, and although James was not mentioned in his stepfather's will, he was soon able to 'borrow' a considerable sum from his widowed mother, to help fend off his creditor and stave off bankruptcy.

In October 1846 Rush had advertised in *The Times* for a governess to look after his children. The girl Rush favoured was a young lady named Emily Sandford, aged about twenty-five. Rush convinced Emily and her parents that he was a polite, respectable and God-fearing man and, at first, everyone thought how fortunate Emily was to secure such a position. Emily moved into Stanfield Hall Farm and soon Rush had inveigled the girl into his arms with a promise of marriage. In 1847 – probably to avoid tongues wagging and ensure his past misbehaviour or current financial pressures did not come to the ears of his new paramour – Rush obtained lodgings for Emily at 2 Mylne Street, Islington, London where he was able to visit her under the guise of an 'uncle'. It was at the Islington residence that Rush arranged a meeting between the aggrieved claimants to Stanfield Hall – Thomas Jermy, John Larner and his son. At the meeting Rush assured them he would do everything in his power to rectify their 'rightful' ownership of the estate. In return, if their claim were proved, he would retain the lease on his two farms for a further twenty-one years. They swore their agreement on a document written by Emily, from a copy supplied by Rush. Emily also witnessed the signatures. It was not to be the last occasion Rush dragged this poor woman into his schemes. A week later, Rush and Emily were back in Norfolk. Rush then concocted some incredible extended leases and mortgages on his Felmingham and Stanfield Hall Farms, drew up the documents, and cajoled Emily into copying them and 'witnessing' the forged signature of Isaac Jermy. Rush and Emily then took up residence as master and mistress at Potash Farm.

In the meantime, Mr Isaac Jermy was residing in Great Yarmouth, but he made sure to keep well informed on the machinations of the errant Rush, who was behind in his payments. And as a consequence of this, Jermy took Rush to court for breach of contract. Jermy's subsequent victory, which was followed by further financial penalisation, drove Rush to express his rage through a defamatory pamphlet, entitled *Report of, and Comments on, a Trial at Norwich Assizes, March 1848, for Breaches of Covenant, said to be Committed by J.B. Rush. And a case, Jermy v. Jermy, or who is the Rightful Owner of Stanfield Hall and Felmingham Estates*. The pamphlet has been described as 'singularly rancorous', and in it Rush made such scurrilous claims as: 'This fellow Jermy has no right to this Stanfield property, he knows it, and he knows I know it well.' Rush goes on to describe Isaac Jermy's behaviour as 'villainous and disgraceful', and attributing his own downfall to Jermy, states there was 'no reason why I should be ruined in character by this villain, as well as my property being swallowed up by him'. Rush was lucky Jermy did not sue for libel, but the latter must have known Rush was financially crippled, and indeed, Rush declared himself bankrupt in May 1848.

W. Teignmouth Shore, the editor of 'Trial of J. Blomfield Rush' in the classic *Notable British Trials* series, eloquently sums up the dire situation Rush was in by November 1848:

> Pecuniarily Rush was in extremis [. . .] He would shortly have to pay his landlord the mortgage on Potash Farm etc., a sum which he could not possibly raise [. . .] He possessed documents from Thomas Jermy and

John Larner, which if they should succeed in their claim to the Stanfield Hall and Felmingham estates would establish him again in security [. . .] He hated Isaac Jermy [. . .] Also, he held the forged agreements between Isaac Jermy and himself, which would be valueless unless the former died within a few days.

To be precise, the loan on Potash Farm was due for settlement on 30 November 1848. On the night of Tuesday 28 November 1848, a telegraph was received by Norwich City Police, stating that Mr Isaac Jermy and his son had been murdered. Chief Constable Peter Yarrington started immediately for Wymondham by train, leaving orders for men to follow. Norwich Police constables were mustered, a number of them armed, and despatched in conveyances to Stanfield Hall. In the account of the crime published by Bacon & Kinnebrook they added: 'Through every line in the kingdom a description was telegraphed of Rush – a curious fact, as no whisper of suspicion as to who was the murderer had been conveyed to Norwich.' Upon arrival at Wymondham Chief Constable Yarrington was sought out by a clerk from the office of Messrs Mitchell & Clarke, solicitors of Wymondham, who stated he had orders to take the Chief Constable to Felmingham, where he would find Rush.

At Stanfield Hall the scene was one of 'utter dismay' and the story of the night's events soon unfurled (Author's Note: in order to differentiate between Isaac Jermy, the Recorder of Norwich, and his son Isaac Jermy Jermy, I shall follow the convention in use at the time and refer to Jermy Snr as Recorder Jermy).

Between 8.15pm and 8.30pm Isaac Jermy Jermy (aged twenty-nine), his wife Sophie, and Isabella, one of Recorder Jermy's daughters (aged about fourteen), were in the drawing room about to sit down at the card table for a game of piquet. Recorder Jermy had, as was his habit after dinner, gone from the dining room to the entrance porch in front of the Hall to take the evening air. A gunshot was heard and the butler, James Watson, came out of his pantry near the front entrance to investigate. Just as he reached the turn of the passage, to his horror, he was confronted by the figure of 'a man in a dark cloak, of lowish stature, and stout, apparently with a mask on his face and something on his head'. The figure pushed the slightly built butler to one side, and as he did so the butler noticed what he be believed to be 'two pistols, one in each hand'. Fearing for his life, Watson cowered at his pantry door as the figure strode on, dropping two papers as he did so.

Young Isaac Jermy Jermy also heard the shots and had run out of the drawing room, across the staircase hall, to the door of the passage. Watson saw the cloaked man draw back a pace, level his gun at Mr Jermy Jermy and shoot him through the right breast at a distance of about 3ft, causing his body to fall backwards onto the mat of the staircase hall. The assassin then crossed

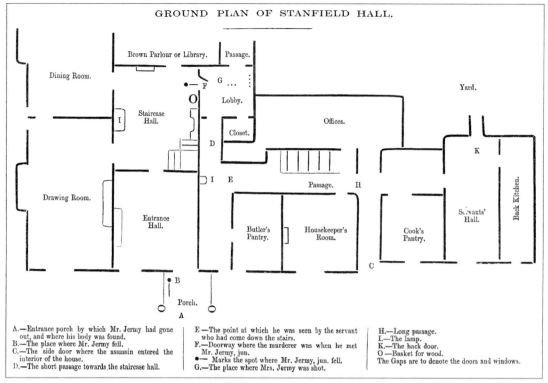

GROUND PLAN OF STANFIELD HALL.

Brown Parlour or Library. Passage.

Dining Room.

Yard.

F

G ...

O

Lobby.

Staircase Hall.

I

Offices.

Closet.

D

K

I E

Passage. H

Drawing Room.

Entrance Hall.

Butler's Pantry.

Housekeeper's Room.

Cook's Pantry.

Servants' Hall.

Back Kitchen.

C

B

Porch.

A

A.—Entrance porch by which Mr. Jermy had gone out, and where his body was found.
B.—The place where Mr. Jermy fell.
C.—The side door where the assassin entered the interior of the house.
D.—The short passage towards the staircase hall.

E.—The point at which he was seen by the servant who had come down the stairs.
F.—Doorway where the murderer was when he met Mr. Jermy, jun.
●— Marks the spot where Mr. Jermy, jun. fell.
G.—The place where Mrs. Jermy was shot.

H.—Long passage.
I.—The lamp.
K.—The back door.
O —Basket for wood.
The Gaps are to denote the doors and windows.

A ground plan of Stanfield Hall.

the hall to the dining room, the door of which was ajar. Upon hearing the second shot Mrs Jermy Jermy rushed out of the drawing room. She was horrified to see her husband lying on his back in a spreading pool of blood. She ran into the small square passage calling for Watson and the other servants, where she met the housemaid, Eliza Chastney, who had heard the shots and run to her mistress. Eliza threw her left arm around her mistress's waist and took her right hand in her own. As Eliza later testified, she said:

'My dear mistress, what is the matter?' She was going back towards the staircase hall. I also went, and when I got as far as the staircase hall – there I saw Mr Isaac Jermy Jermy lying on the floor. I then saw a man coming from the dining room, and he had what appeared to be a short gun or pistol in the right hand [raised] up to the shoulder. He levelled it and shot me. I did not fall directly. Another shot followed at once, and I saw my mistress's arm twirl about. My mistress left me and ran upstairs. I twisted round several times and fell down. I gave three violent shrieks, and I said I was going to die, and no one would come and help me.

The cover of *Famous Crimes* depicts a fanciful image of the shooting of Recorder Jermy.

In fact two shots were fired in quick succession, the first catching Mrs Jermy Jermy's upper arm, the second wounding Eliza Chastney in the groin and thigh. The murderer then made his exit by the side door.

After medical examination it was thought Eliza had received 'a whole charge' that caused a compound fracture of the bone. The wound to Mrs Jermy Jermy's arm eventually resulted in amputation. Eliza Chastney had briefly passed out: the next face she recalled seeing was that of Watson the butler, who had dashed across to see what had happened to her, and then ran out of the house to summon assistance. Eliza testified that she:

> awoke at the bottom of the staircase [. . .] I saw the head and shoulders of the man who shot me. There was something remarkable in the head; it was flat on the top – the hair set out bushy – and he was wide shouldered. I formed a belief at the time who the man was, I have no doubt in my own mind about it.

She identified the man as James Blomfield Rush. Despite the disguise she qualified her belief: 'Mr Rush has a way of carrying his head which can't be mistaken. No person ever came to Stanfield with such an appearance, beside himself.'

Watson ran to the nearest farmhouse, that of Mr Gower. Martha Read, the cook, had fled to the coach house with young Sophie Jermy and the coachman had dived into the moat at the back of the house, swum across and run to summon assistance from Mr Colman at Hall Farm. The first to return with assistance was Watson with Mr Gower and his two sons. They were soon joined by Mr Colman and Mr Skoulding, the Surgeon from Wymondham. Word had been sent to call the Surgeon, the Local Magistrate, the County Constabulary and Norwich City Police. Local magistrates and law officials led by Mr Cann were rapidly on the scene. By the lamps of the Surgeon's gig they saw the lifeless body of 59-year-old Recorder Jermy lying in the porch. The bodies of Recorder Jermy and his son were then removed to the dining room. Recorder Jermy was found to have a mortal wound to his left breast; so close had the shot been delivered, the clothes all around the wound were badly singed. The corpses of father and son were laid side by side on the carpet.

The first police officer – Constable George Pont of Norfolk County Police – arrived at Stanfield Hall at about 9.20pm. He recovered five 'slugs' (irregular sized pieces of lead shot) from near the body of Mr Jermy Snr on the staircase hall side. The main contingent of Norwich City Police arrived between one and two in the morning and joined the County constables watching Potash Farm, making a cordon around the building. About 3am a dog was heard to give a slight bark at the back of the farm. A young lad, named Solomon Savory, employed by Rush was seen coming from a lean-to at the rear of the farm and was then seen to go from the back kitchen to the stable. He met PC Pont in the yard, who sent the boy back with a message to Rush that Mr Cann the magistrate wished to speak with him urgently. Upon receiving the message Rush promptly came down into the kitchen and unbolted the door. PC John Morter was first in, followed by PC Pont and PC Stephen Amis. Pont said: 'You must consider yourself my prisoner, on suspicion of murdering the two Mr Jermys last night.' Rush replied to the charge: 'The two Jermys murdered?' At the same time Rush was handcuffed. Distracted by this, Rush said: 'I don't like these', but went on to comment of the murders: 'God knows I am clear of that.'

Rush called up to Emily Sandford, who came down and was startled by the scene. Rush proclaimed ignorance of any misdeeds and asked a somewhat bewildered Emily to make breakfast. PCs Pont, Amis and Morter then conducted a preliminary search of the house with Rush. Morter found a black cloak lying on Rush's bed. Two double-barrelled shotguns were also recovered. Pont remarked to Rush: 'You used to have pistols.' Rush replied: 'I used to have, but have none now.' Rush asked what time the murders had been committed. His question was not answered, but a few seconds later, Rush said one of the policemen had told him a little after eight. The arresting constables agreed that no one had been heard to mention the time of the

"YOU MUST CONSIDER YOURSELF MY PRISONER."

The members of the Norwich and Norfolk police forces make their entrance and arrest Rush.

crime. As Rush set about eating his breakfast, somewhat encumbered by the handcuffs, he said:

> I am accused of murdering Jermy and his son, but that fellow Clarke has done this – it is he that has caused me to be suspected, but you and Savory can clear me, for he (Savory) washed my boots at half past five and you know I did not go out again until after tea.

Pausing, Rush asked Emily: 'Have you been asked any questions?' 'Yes,' she replied, 'that stout man asked me if you went out last evening, and I said you went out at eight o'clock for about quarter of an hour.' Rush retorted: 'I was not more than ten minutes, and you know I had my slipper shoes on.' Rush went on blustering for some time about hearing a constable state the time the murders were committed. After breakfast Rush was removed under police guard by gig to Wymondham Bridewell.

In the daylight an immediate search for potential clues – especially the murder weapons in the Hall and surroundings – was instigated. As news of the murders broke there was a great deal of public and press interest. A contemporary account stated:

> This excitement continued for not just one day but many; and although it is not to be denied, that the late Recorder of Norwich, from his bluntness and peculiarity of manner, was not a popular man [. . .] there was no inhabitant, possessing the smallest particle of feeling, who was not anxious to aid, by any means, in the discovery of the assassin.

Back at Stanfield Hall a number of labourers were even employed in cutting a drain, and then Shalders' pumps were brought in to draw off water from the moat, in case the weapons had been thrown in. The 'papers' that Watson saw dropped by the disguised killer were recovered and found to be half a sheet of foolscap pasted onto two board covers from a book. Both bore identical messages written in 'a large printed style', stating:

> There are seven of us here, three of us outside, and four inside the hall, all armed as you see us two. If any of you servants offer to leave the premises or to follow, you will be shot dead. Therefore, all of you keep in the servants' hall and you nor anyone else will take any arme [sic], for we are only come to take possession of the Stanfield Hall property.
> THOMAS JERMY, the owner

Investigations and searches continued over the following days. On Friday 1 December, Superintendent Henry Hubbersty conducted a search of Potash Farm. In Rush's bedroom he found a box in the closet containing, among other things, a widow's cap, some old loose papers, a black wig with a pair of mustachios and whiskers attached, a black woman's frontlet wig with long hair attached, and a travelling cap. In a later search by Superintendent Witherspoon the forged deeds witnessed by Emily Sandford were discovered beneath joists in a closet.

On Thursday 30 November, summonses were issued for a jury to hold an inquest at Wymondham at the King's Head. The jury returned a verdict of 'wilful murder' against James Blomfield Rush and the Coroner issued his warrant accordingly. After magistrates' hearings on 13 and 14 December 1848 they committed Rush to trial, and he was removed to await his appearance at the Assizes in Norwich Castle Gaol. Emily Sandford was detained by the want of sureties, as well as from her own desires, in Wymondham Bridewell, as was the lad Solomon Savory, also for want of sureties.

The bodies of Recorder Jermy and his son were laid to rest on 5 December, enclosed in plain oak coffins, made from a tree grown on the Stanfield estate. Under the direction of the Undertaker, Mr Blakely, each coffin was contained in its own hearse, followed by three mourning coaches with the tenantry following on horseback. The shops of Wymondham were closed during the time of the funeral procession and the window blinds of private houses were pulled down, many local people lining the route. Wymondham Abbey was packed with people from the area, many of them local farmers. The bodies were met at the north entrance of the church by the Revd David Jones, the Curate, and after due service, the coffins were finally conveyed to their newly erected vault on the south side of the church.

As Rush's trial approached, his unequivocal denial of all murder allegations, the failure to recover the murder weapons, and fears over the precarious conditions of Mrs Jermy Jermy and Eliza Chastney, led to concerns for securing a sound case against Rush. It was at this time, during the ongoing search for the murder weapon, that Charles Dickens recorded a visit to Stanfield Hall on 12 January 1849, and did not reserve his concerns about the way the search was being conducted:

> We arrived between the Hall and Potash Farm, as the search was going on for the pistol in a manner so consummately stupid, that there was nothing on earth to prevent any of Rush's labourers from accepting five pounds from Rush junior to find the weapon and give it to him.

A fast-loading double-barrelled blunderbuss thought likely to have been one of the murder weapons was found after the trial on 19 May, under a dung heap in the yard near Potash Farm.

Emily Sandford was about eight months pregnant with Rush's child when she visited him at Norwich Castle Gaol in late December 1848. It appears that during their meeting Rush became frustrated and probably feared that Emily

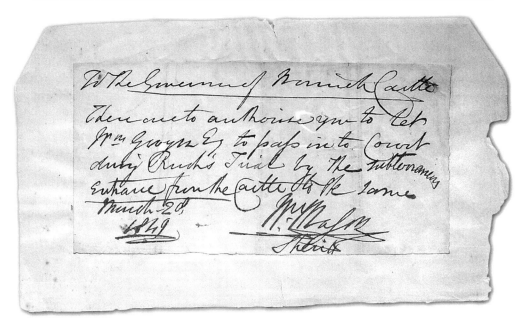

A sheriff's ticket to admit the lucky owner to a prime seat at the trial of James Rush.
(Stewart P. Evans Archive)

The palanquin containing Eliza Chastney, severely wounded in the Stanfield Hall slayings, is carried to the Shirehall by Norfolk police constables, escorted by officers of Norwich City Police.

would not lie for him and flew into a violent rage, in which he even cursed the child she was carrying. Despite his sending her letters begging forgiveness, she wanted her conscience to be clear. Emily Sandford gave a voluntary statement on 13 February 1849, said to have been written in the latter days of her confinement bearing Rush's child and signed between the opening waves of pain from labour, in the presence of Wymondham solicitor Mr J.S. Cann. Emily told all she knew and could remember of the events leading up to and during the night of 28 November 1848. In a long and detailed statement, the salient points she stated were that Rush had claimed he was worried about poachers and had taken to going out of an evening with his guns. Emily had become increasingly concerned by Rush's behaviour and made a point of asking him if there was something more than poachers for which he was desirous of going out. He replied cryptically: 'You could not wish to know now, but you will know another time.' Crucially, Emily confessed she could not vouch for Rush's whereabouts at the crucial time on the fateful night the Jermys were killed.

The trial opened on Thursday 29 March 1849, before Baron Rolfe. Rush had arrogantly turned down offers of legal counsel and opted to defend himself. The prosecution was led by Mr Sergeant Byles with Mr Prendergast and Mr Evans. Rush was often belligerent and attempted to intimidate the prosecution witnesses The press and broadsheet sellers were having a field day, with extended accounts and illustrated supplements, while the large crowds that gathered in front of the Shirehall confirmed intense public interest in the case.

The drama was heightened by the arrival of injured housemaid Eliza Chastney to give evidence. Her injuries were such that she was bedridden and still in considerable pain. A bed had been specially constructed to be carried by men in a manner similar to that of a sedan chair, except this had a tent-like canvas canopy and curtains. In this palanquin she was carried from Stanfield Hall to Norwich in relays, with a stop every 40yds. Escorted by County Police to Harford Bridges, the cortege was met by a large body of City Police, under the direct command of Chief Constable Yarrington. The Norwich constables formed a line in front and a line behind, with the County constables at the side, in the event of there being 'eager curiosity or improper conduct'. And thus the unique procession brought the star witness to the first day of the trial, and from her canopied bed this brave young lady repeated her account of the night, confidently identifying Rush as the perpetrator. Eliza's evidence and her identification of Rush by his build, gait and shape of head, were corroborated by Watson the butler and Martha Read the cook.

The second day of the trial, and a large proportion of the third, saw Emily Sandford take the stand. As Rush's mistress she attracted a great deal of public interest and curiosity. Rush, however, was disturbed by her appearance and 'betrayed unusual excitement'. He addressed the Judge, saying he wished

Eliza Chastney giving her
evidence from the palanquin.
Rush can be seen in the dock
on the right.

Emily Sandford and the matron
of Wymondham Bridewell,
drawn from life, in court.

to make an observation, but the Judge objected, to which Rush retorted: 'I have a higher power than you, my Lord, and I say to this witness, that I am innocent of this charge.' Emily, dressed in her best Sunday clothes, looked slender and somewhat vulnerable as she spoke from the witness box. She enlarged on her previous statement by revealing that Rush had left Potash Farmhouse on the night of the murder at 7.30pm and told her to fasten the door behind him. She saw nothing more of Rush until between 9 and 9.30pm, when he announced his return with a rap on the door. He passed through the parlour and went straight upstairs without a light saying, 'Take the top of the fire off and come to bed.' Emily described him as looking 'pale, ill and agitated'. She asked what was the matter – had anything happened? Rush replied: 'No, nothing, if you hear any inquiries for me say I was out only ten minutes.' Later on, in the small hours of the night, Rush went to her bedroom and started talking in an excited and disturbed manner: 'You must be firm,' he pressed, 'if anybody asks how long I was out, say ten minutes.'

Her life with Rush, her blind trust in him, and the documents he gave her to sign and witness, were sensitively and expertly explored by Mr Prendergast for the prosecution. The public had mixed feelings about Emily: in some press reports she was painted as something of an accomplice; but after her clear and honest testimony, and after being subjected to the bullying tactics of Rush in his long-winded and fatuous cross-examination (which lasted over seven and a half hours), public opinion swung in favour of this impressionable young lady.

Emily was followed by a series of witnesses who testified to Rush's animosity towards Recorder Jermy. The letters gummed on the book covers were disposed of as crude attempts to deflect suspicion. The witnesses for the prosecution were concluded with testimonies from the arresting officer and the constables who accompanied him. On the fifth day of the trial (Tuesday 3 April) Rush, looking every bit the melodrama villain – bulky, aggressive, conceited, and dressed completely in black – lumbered over from the dock to the witness box to deliver his defence. He was to speak, in total, for a marathon fourteen hours. More blustering fabrications, half-truths and barefaced lies typified his address, with sanctimonious intercessions such as 'God Almighty will protect me', and 'God Almighty knows I am innocent'. His five witnesses were hardly worthwhile, and even damning. Notable among them was Maria Blanchflower, a nurse at Stanfield Hall. She stated she had seen the disguised murderer but did not recognise the figure as Rush, despite having run past within a few feet of him. Rush asked: 'Did you pass *me* [author italics] quickly?' An unfortunate slip of the tongue – especially in open court!

The sixth day of the trial saw the last of the defence witnesses, including the fateful and telling exchange between Rush and Nurse Blanchflower. The prosecution and Judge summed up the last few days eloquently and succinctly. There had been a vast amount of evidence to digest, but Rush had not helped himself with his convoluted and often irrelevant cross-examinations.

The weight of evidence pressed against him, and Rush stood little chance of acquittal. The jury returned their verdict after just ten minutes' deliberation – 'Guilty'. Rush burst forth: 'My lord, I am innocent of that, thank God Almighty.' When asked why the death sentence should not be pronounced upon him, the prisoner remained silent.

Baron Rolfe assumed the black cap and pulled no punches in a tirade against Rush, his vitriol well evinced in the following:

> There is no one that has witnessed your conduct during the trial, and heard the evidence disclosed against you, that will not feel with me, when I tell you that you must quit this world by an ignominious death, an object of unmitigating abhorrence to everyone.

During this final pronouncement Rush spoke once only, when the Judge chided him for not making good his promise to Miss Sandford, for if he had, she may well have invoked her legal right to refuse to testify against her husband. Rush, petty to the bitter end, replied: 'I did not make any promise.' Rush said no more. Sentence of death was passed; he apparently regained his composure, and was removed from the dock 'with a smile and an unfeeling observation' to the condemned cell of Norwich Castle Gaol, there to await his fate.

The behaviour of Rush in Norwich Gaol was much the same before, during and after trial and sentence. He adopted the airs and phraseology of piety apparent in a devoutly religious man, but in Rush's case, without the dignity. His act fooled no one. The men of God did not judge and listened to Rush in his hours of need and 'sincere' protestations of innocence, but after Rush's execution a sketch of his demeanour and conduct was provided by the Prison Chaplain, the Revd James Brown, Hon. Canon to the Cathedral and Minister of St Andrews. His opening comments sum up his opinion:

> Rush, from the first moment of his apprehension, undertook a character which he was unable to support. He assumed the lofty and confident bearing of innocence; but he so unnaturally overacted his part, as to enable the most casual observer to see through the flimsy veil which he attempted to throw over his real feelings.

Assiduously attending every religious service, reading the Bible and demanding regular attendance by the prison chaplain, Rush requested his Holy Sacrament to be administered to him in private, but as he refused to be penitent or offer a confession for his crime, this request was refused. Displeased with the Prison Chaplain, Rush requested attendance from two other ministers known to him, namely the Revd W.W. Andrews of Felmingham and the Revd C.J. Blake of Ketteringham. Rush also became increasingly belligerent towards these men, as they could not promise to intercede on his behalf.

Rush had ensured he ate well in captivity: refusing the prison food (although who could blame him), he ordered his meals in from a nearby inn. In a letter to Mr Leggatt of the Bell Inn dated 24 March 1849, revealing much of Rush's pernickety character, the condemned man laid out his requirements:

Sir,

You will oblige me by sending my breakfast this morning, and my dinner about the time your family have theirs, send anything you like *except beef*; and I shall like cold meat as well as hot, and meal bread, and tea in a pint mug, if with a cover on the better. I will trouble you to provide for me now, if you please, till after my trial, and if you could get a small sucking pig in the market today, and roast it for me on the Monday, I should like that cold as well as hot after Monday, and it would always be in readiness for me [. . .] Have the pig cooked the same as you usually have, and send plenty of plum sauce with it. Mr Pinson will pay you for what I have of you. By complying with the above,

You will very much oblige,
Your humble and obedient servant,
James B. Rush

The execution of James Rush was set for noon on Saturday 21 April 1849. Rush prepared himself that morning with a breakfast of 'a little thin gruel', followed by a visit to the prison chapel. The service finished at 11.40am and the Prison Chaplain, seconded by Revd Andrews, urged Rush to repent. But he only became irritated, declaring: 'God knows my heart; He is my judge, and you have prejudged me [. . .] the real criminal will be known in two years.' Rush then lost his temper, and upon hearing the prisoner's raised voice, the Governor, Mr Pinson, personally removed Rush from the chapel. Rush cooled himself down by washing his face, hands, and neck with water from the pump in the prison yard.

From the prison yard Rush was conducted inside to the pinioning room, where he would meet his executioner, William Calcraft. Upon seeing Calcraft, Rush gruffly asked: 'Is that the man who is to perform this duty?' to which Mr Pinson replied he was. Calcraft asked Rush to sit down and began to pinion his hands. Rush said with a shrug: 'This don't go easy; I don't want the cord to hurt me.' Calcraft loosened the restraint a little and Rush confirmed he was comfortable and joined the procession to the gallows.

The morning of the execution was cold, dismal and cheerless. Small groups had collected on Norwich Castle hill from an early hour. Most of these early arrivals were members of the farming community. A contemporary account stated:

They eyed, at a respectful distance, the dreadful apparatus of death, and in little knots, with bated breath, talked over the fate of the wretched man, whom many of them no doubt known and bargained with, and whose occupation in life had been similar to their own.

As the hour of execution approached, the sun broke through the clouds and shone down as a crowd of thousands of men, women and children assembled to view the spectacle. Shortly before noon numbers swelled further, as a large crowd arrived from the specially chartered trains from London and across East Anglia. The usual viewing points bulged to capacity, housetops – even one of

THE EXECUTION OF

JAMES BLOOMFIELD RUSH

AT

NORWICH CASTLE, APRIL 23rd., 1849,

For the murder of Isaac Jermy, Esq., the Recorder of Norwich, and his son, I. Jermy Jermy, Esq.,

AT

STANFIELD HALL.

Between 11 and 12 o'clock the bell of St Peter's, Mancroft, tolled the death knell of the criminal. When conducted to the turnkey's room to be pinioned he met Calcraft, whereupon he said to Mr Pinson " Is this the man that is to do the business?" The reply was " Yes." When he was pinioned he shrugged up his shoulders, saying " This don't go easy ; it's too tight."

Within two or three minutes after 12 o'clock the mournful cavalcade proceeded from the interior of the Castle to the spot on which the gibbet was erected. The chaplain, who headed the procession, read, as he passed along, part of the burial service.

When the procession left the Castle gate to proceed to the gibbet, Rush presented a most melancholy and dejected appearance. He was dressed in a plain suit of black, wearing no neck-hankerchief. His shirt collar was turned down. For about twenty yards he walked with a firm unwavering step, but in a moment afterwards he raised his pinioned hands to his face and trembled violently. He then removed his hands from his face, and turning up his eyes to heaven, assumed the attitude of penitence and prayer. On reaching the gallows the rev. chaplain offered up a prayer. While this prayer was being read the condemned convict seemed to be deeply impressed with the awful character of his situation. Immediately on the close of the prayer he beckoned to Mr Pinson, the governor of the Castle, when the following brief conversation ensued :

Rush : Mr Pinson, I have a last request to make to you. It is that the bolt may be withdrawn while the chaplain is reading the benediction—" The grace of our Lord Jesus Christ, and the love of God, and the fellowship of the Holy Ghost, be with us all, evermore."

Mr Pinson : I will communicate your wish to the chaplain, and I have no doubt it will be attended to.

The hangman then placed the unhappy convict under the beam on which he was to hang, and affixed the fatal rope around his neck. Rush said, " For God's sake give me rope enough. Don't be in a hurry ; take your time." Then moving his head about, he said " Put the knot a little higher up, don't hurry." The rev. chaplain proceeded with the prayers, and on arriving at the words " The grace of our Lord Jesus Christ," &c., Calcraft withdrew the bolt, the platform went down, and all was over. His death was greeted with loud applause by an immense crowd who had assembled to witness the execution.

Good people listen unto my song,
And girls to whom honest hearts belong,
Pay great attention to what I say,
And by the wicked be not led astray.

Poor Emily Sandford was learned well,
Yet mark what to her fatal lot befel,
The serpent's tongue caused the tears to gush,
For she was betrayed by James Bloomfield Rush.

She begged most pleadingly to be his wife,
And lived with him a most unhappy life,
And though the hot tears down her cheeks did flow
The monster heeded not Miss Sandford's woe.

But seeing that she now was ruined quite,
She stood upon her feet in female might,
And with her pale hand stretched towards his face
Said, " God will curse thee for my deep disgrace."

Forboding were the words Miss Sandford said,
For murderous thoughts were in the wretch's head.
He set to work, and speedily did plan,
The death of servants, husband, wife, and son.

A five barrelled pistol he soon did buy,
And then a mask upon his face did try,
Put on his hat and cloak and pistols drew,
Within its fold a bloody deed to do.

For Stanfield Hall he quick did start,
And old Squire Jermy he shot through the heart !
And while the grey-hair'd man lay bleeding there,
He shot his son and lovely wife so fair.

Eliza Chestney to her Mistress ran,
Saying, " dearest mistress, who is this man ?"
And, while she pressed her mistress to her heart,
A bullet pierced in a dangerous part.

James Bloomfield Rush was then to prison sent,
Miss Sandford against him a witness went,
She was well avenged—for on the gallows high,
The base seducer was condemned to die !

The Judge soon told him that his race was run,—
That he must die for murderous deeds he'd done,
To use the time that yet on earth was given,
In making peace with his God in heaven.

O had you witness'd the parting hour,
Of this wretched man and his nine children dear,
Your hearts would break to think that they might see,
Their father hung upon a gallows tree.

J. Harkness, Printer, Preston.

A broadsheet sold at the execution of James Rush.

'Put the thing a little higher' – the last moments of James Rush on the scaffold in front of Norwich Castle, 21 April 1849.

the city's square-towered churches – being packed with people eager for a glimpse of the final act of the Stanfield Hall tragedy.

Broadsheet sellers and the hawkers of hot pies, potatoes and drinks had a roaring trade – as did the pickpockets! The short space between the Castle Prison gate and the scaffold was lined on one side by the magistrates of the county and representatives of the press on the other. Shortly after the appointed hour the great door opened and the Sheriff's entourage, attended by javelin men, led the solemn procession. Colonel Oakes, the Chief Constable of the County Police, followed; succeeded by the chaplain, reading aloud the appropriate portion of the burial service. The Chaplain was followed by Rush, attended on one side by Mr Pinson, the Governor of the Castle Gaol, and Calcraft the Executioner on the other, with a number of the turnkeys following. The bell of St Peter Mancroft tolling the death knell, the procession almost moving in time with each slow, mournful chime. As they strode out, Rush's tread and composure was remarkably firm. Rush was attired in the same black suit and patent leather boots he had worn for his trial; the collar of his shirt – remarked upon as being 'scrupulously clean' – was turned over for the purpose of freely adjusting the noose. His head bare, Rush's

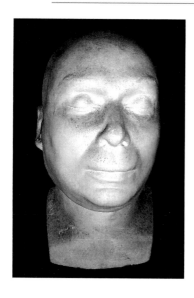

The death mask of James Rush. Eerily, the indentation of the rope can still be seen around his corpulent neck. *(Stewart P. Evans Archive)*

features were keenly observed: it was noted they had undergone no perceptible change since his trial – 'perhaps a little paler, but his determined expression had not changed.'

Upon seeing the scaffold Rush lifted his eyes to Heaven, and raising his pinioned hands as far as he could, shook his head mournfully from side to side once or twice. He was led up the steps of the gallows and placed under the fatal beam. An eyewitness recorded:

The wretched creature looked for an instant on the vast mass of spectators, whose earnest gaze was upon him and on every movement he made, and then turned himself round and faced the castle – his back being towards the populace.

Clearly Rush could not resist one last defiant gesture! He shook hands with the Governor, then Calcraft drew the white hood over Rush's head, and having fastened the rope to the beam, set about adjusting the noose around Rush's neck. Unable to resist a last whinge, a voice snapped at the Executioner from under the hood: 'This does not go easy! Put the thing a little higher – take your time – don't be in a hurry!' These were to be Rush's last words. As the Chaplain read the passage requested by Rush ('The Grace of our Lord Jesus Christ . . . ') the signal was given and the bolt was drawn, releasing the gallows trapdoor, 'and the scene of life closed upon this malefactor, almost without a struggle.'

The crowd maintained an eerie silence, excepting a few faint shrieks as the trap fell. The sound of the falling trap and the tightening rope was audible over some considerable distance.

Rush was left to hang for the obligatory hour, to serve – as contemporary accounts state – as 'a caution to the world, beware lest you fall'. When the body was taken down it was removed to the prison on a wheeled litter. In the afternoon Rush's head was shaved and a 'death mask' cast by Mr Bianchi of St George's Middle-Street in Norwich. The remains were then buried within the precincts of the prison. According to regulations, no headstone was granted: only a stone tablet bearing his initials and the year of his execution mark the final resting-place of James Blomfield Rush, known to history and infamy as The Stanfield Hall Murderer.

3

THE REPENTANCE OF WILLIAM SHEWARD

Norwich 1851

On 21 June 1851 twelve-year-old Charlie Johnson was out on a fine, sunny day, taking his dog for a walk along Lakenham Lane. Suddenly, the dog bounded off over a small plantation at Bracondale, on the scent of what his owner thought might be a rabbit. The dog stopped short and started to have a good snuffle, then bounded back with what appeared to be a chunk of discarded meat – and not a very good cut at that – clasped in its jaws like a trophy. Charlie took little notice of the object carried in the mouth of his faithful friend. The dog seemed pleased with his find and, tail up, he led the way home. When they arrived the boy took a second look at the 'trophy', as the dog dropped it between his paws and began licking it – the object was a human hand! The boy's father immediately wrapped the hand in paper and took it to the Police Station. Young Charlie was called to the Police Station and was asked to show a constable exactly where he had found it.

Another couple of lads, Dickie Fryer and Bobby Field, were playing at Mr Merry's house, whose garden bounded St Peter Southgate Church-Alley. Just before they reached the alley the boys found a hand lying in the long grass on the border of Mr Merry's garden. On closer examination it was a left hand with the ring finger cut off. Another lad, Thomas Dent, was out with his dog and discovered a human foot on Martineau Lane. A few days later, on 24 June, Samuel Moore, a nightwatchman, came across a piece of flesh in Mr Stroulger's field on St Augustine's Road. PCs Flaxman, Noller and Skalt were immediately sent to search the area and recovered sections of human breast, clearly that of a female. Another section of breast and a navel were found by William Neave near Reynold's Mill. Over the next four weeks Norwich City and Norfolk County Police organised major searches of grassy areas around the city, assisted by public volunteers: even young Charlie Johnson joined in with his keen dog, and found two more pieces of flesh on the Hellesdon Road. And yet more parts were recovered by police and public on a field called 'Iron Box' on Green Hills, off Hangman's Lane (now Heigham Road), and on Alder Carr at Trowse Eye.

HIS DOG BROUGHT HIM A HUMAN FOOT.

Thomas Dent's dog brings him a very unwelcome trophy.

John Walter Sales of Bull Close was employed to clean out the cockeys (small streams often channelled and used as drains around the city) in Bishopgate Street. As he lifted the grate to empty the cockey around 300yds from Tabernacle Street, opposite the 'Old Lady's Hospital' (*sic*), he was startled to find that it appeared to be filled with blood. His father worked with him, and said they had just better get on with the job of lifting the 'soil' onto their cart. They had heard about the body parts found around the city and shared their concerns with PC Sturgess, who came to inspect the sludge removed from the drain to the heap on Bull Close Road, where human entrails, more grisly flesh, and part of a breast with a nipple still attached were discovered.

The unenviable task of assembling the body parts fell to Police Sergeant Edward Peck. A former butcher, all his former skills were required in identifying which pieces were human and which were discarded meat and mutton bones brought to the police by well-meaning members of the public, garnered into vigilance by press coverage, police notices and gossip. Within four weeks of searching, the human body parts he received amounted to: two hands, two feet, a thigh bone, lower leg bones, parts of a pelvis, some vertebrae and a grisly selection of flesh, strips of skin and muscle.

The portions of flesh were preserved in wine and examined with the bones at the same time by a team of three local surgeons: Mr Nichols, Mr Dalrymple and Mr Norgate. They thought several pieces of flesh were not human, but agreed most of the bones had been correctly identified. They agreed the remains were those of an adult female about twenty-five years of age – but their assessment of the victim's age later proved inaccurate.

The method of dissection exercised on the victim did not evince an experienced medical hand – or even that of a skilled butcher. For example, the pelvis had been sawn through roughly, 'partly in one direction and then in another and then snapped asunder'. A thought was promulgated that rather than a horrible murder, the body parts had been distributed about the city as a sick prank by medical students, who had stolen a cadaver.

A young girl named Mary Villings had been reported missing at the time, and several people came forward to state they had family members missing, after a series of posters were put up around the city asking for assistance in

CITY OF NORWICH

SUPPOSED MURDER

Several parts of a human body belonging to a person supposed to have been recently murdered, and to be that of a young female between the ages of sixteen and twenty-six years having been, within the last few days found in the environs of the city of Norwich.

Information is requested to be given to the Chief Constable at the Police Office, Guildhall, Norwich, of all females who may have been recently missing together with any particulars which may lead to the detecting of the person or persons who committed such supposed murder.

The portions of the body already found comprise the right hand and foot and several bones, with numerous pieces of skin and flesh. Further search is making for the head and remaining parts of the body.

H. WOODCOCK,
Mayor.

The poster, distributed across Norwich, which sought an identity for the body parts found around the city.

identifying the remains of 'a person supposed to have been recently murdered, and to be that of a young female between the ages of sixteen and twenty-six.' But no one could identify the collection of grisly remains for certain, and as no head had been recovered – nor anything else that could be described as a distinguishing feature – the investigation made little progress. Thus, with no victim or suspect identified, the sensational accounts in the papers ran out of steam and interest in the case waned. A month or so after the last body parts had been discovered Sergeant Peck was instructed to bury the remains in two vessels in a vault under the Guildhall and throw lime on top.

To all intents and purposes the mystery of the body parts was consigned to history and all but forgotten until almost eighteen years later, when, at about 10.30pm on 1 January 1869, a man in a morose state walked into the South London suburban Police Station on Carter Street, Walworth. Inspector James Davies was on duty and the man addressed him directly: 'I want to speak to you. I have a charge I want to make against myself.' Undoubtedly fed up with the drunks that took up police time over the festive season, Davies responded curtly: 'What is it? Explain yourself.' The man declared: 'Wilful murder of my wife at Norwich.' Davies was not one for time-wasters. He narrowed his eyes and assayed the man, his keen nose sniffing for alcohol: there was none. Davies said: 'Have you considered the serious charge you are making against yourself?' The man replied earnestly: 'Yes, I have. I have kept it for years but can keep it no longer. I left home on Tuesday with the intent to destroy myself with the razor I have in my pocket.' Davies calmly asked the man for

Carter Street police station, Walworth, *c.* 1905.

the razor and he handed it over with no qualms. The man went on falteringly, speaking at intervals between the sobs welling inside him: 'I have been to Chelsea today, and I went yesterday by steamboat, intending to destroy my life, but the Almighty would not let me do it.' Wondering if he was faced with a crank, Inspector Davies suggested again that perhaps the man was under some delusion, but this seemed to harden his resolve to be taken seriously: 'I wish to make the charge in writing.' Davies saw the man was not going to be dissuaded and took down his statement. The man dictated: 'I, William Sheward, charge myself with the wilful murder of my wife . . .'

After signing the declaration Sheward was placed in a cell. Perhaps wondering if he needed to sleep off whatever was troubling him, Inspector Davies left the mysterious confessant to his slumbers. Visiting Sheward in his cell the following morning, Davies enquired: 'Do you remember what you said last night?' Sheward calmly replied: 'Yes, perfectly well.' He went on to give a full confession that told the complete and gruesome story of the tragedy.

The story began when William Sheward (aged twenty-four), a London pawnbroker's assistant, married Martha Francis (aged thirty-nine), a native of Wymondham in Norfolk who was working as a domestic servant, on 28 October 1836 at Greenwich. Despite the age gap, and some fiery arguments, they seemed to rub along well enough. Shortly after their wedding the Shewards stayed with Martha's twin sister and her husband in Wymondham for about four months. More work was to be found in Norwich and over the next two years the couple lived in a number of rented homes in Norwich, William resuming his former occupation as a tailor. William saved money from tailoring and opened his own business as a pawnbroker on St Giles Street. This was not a success, however, and resulted in William being subject to bankruptcy proceedings in 1849. No doubt to avoid seizure of all his assets, William placed a cash box containing the considerable sum of £400 in the care of Mr Christie, a clothier and pawnbroker in Great Yarmouth. Possibly to avoid debt-collectors, landlords or bailiffs, the couple moved to Richmond Hill on Bracondale, then to Ber Street, and finally to 7 Tabernacle Street, in one of the straggling houses then standing opposite the Bishop's Wall, not far from the Great Hospital (most of the Tabernacle Street known to Sheward is today demolished and the roadway, running from St Martin at Palace Plain to the Adam & Eve pub, made part of Bishopgate).

By 1851 Martha was fifty-four and William thirty-nine. As one contemporary account phrased it:

one of the unhappy consequences of such marriages, where there is such an age difference, the younger man was then at an age when all the animal passions are, perhaps, at their zenith, while his wife would be at an age when they had almost probably passed away.

Tabernacle Street in the early twentieth century.

In other words, it was inferred that William was showing improper interest in younger women. This was certainly the opinion of Martha, and her suspicions led to more quarrels: arguments and threats that she would leave William – threats she would utter both in private and in public.

Sheward had been able to withdraw money from Christie upon request. The previous June he had withdrawn £150, but Martha was not satisfied. She could not see why William didn't just bring the whole lot home, and when Christie asked if he could borrow some of the money for his own use, Martha was determined to go to Yarmouth herself and demand the box back.

On Saturday 14 June 1851 Christie asked if Sheward would mind going to Yarmouth on Sunday to pay £10 to a captain of a vessel laden with salt, to enable him to unload on the Monday morning. William rose early on the morning of Sunday the 15th, in preparation for his trip to Yarmouth. While he was shaving at the washstand in their bedroom, Martha opened another argument about bringing the cash box and its contents back. Sheward said he did not think it was possible, to which she snapped: 'You shall not go! I will go to Mr Christie and get the box of money myself and bring it home.' This time she was clearly not to be dissuaded, and one of their fierce arguments soon erupted. Sheward felt his cut-throat razor in his hand, gripping it in rage till his knuckles went white. He could stand no more, and as Sheward later confessed: 'I ran the razor into her throat. She never spoke after. I then covered an apron over her head and went to Yarmouth.'

Ran the razor into her throat.

William Sheward ends the life of his wife Martha by lunging a razor to her throat.

Sheward described what happened next in his frank and detailed condemned cell confession:

I came home that night and slept on the sofa downstairs. On the Monday I went to work and left off at 4pm and went home. The house began to smell very faint. With that I made a fire in the bedroom and commenced to mutilate the body. Kept on until 9.30pm. I then took some portions of the body and threw it away, arriving home at 10.30pm.

41

That night I slept on the sofa again. The next day (Tuesday) went home in the afternoon about 4pm and did the same the same night. Wednesday, went to work as usual, left off early and went home. Carried the portions in a frail basket to another part of the city. Thursday, worked the same and returned early. The head had been put in a saucepan and put on the fire to keep the stench away. I then broke it up and distributed it about Thorpe. Came home and emptied the pail in the cockey in Bishopgate Street with the entrails etc. I then put the hands and feet in the same saucepan in hope they might boil to pieces.

Friday, went to work, and went home early and disposed of all he remains of the body, hands and feet included, because I knew I should not be able to be at home on Saturday until late. On Sunday I burnt all the sheets and nightgown, pillowcases and bed-tick, and all that had any blood about them. The blankets, where there were blood about them, I rent in small pieces and distributed about the city, and made off with everything that had any blood about them. The long hair, on my return from Thorpe, I cut up with a pair of scissors into small pieces, and they blew away as I walked along.

Because all Martha's family lived in Wymondham, and they had little communication between each other anyway, she was not immediately missed. Indeed, any folks who did enquire after Martha were told that she had run off, leaving William penniless: after the couple's public arguments and all her threats to leave, people were hardly surprised, and because the body parts discovered were said to be those of a far younger woman, no one made the connection between the two.

In the November after her murder, Sheward was told Martha's brother had died. The informant, one of Martha's nieces, asked if he would attend the funeral. Sheward declined but the young woman pressed: 'Perhaps my aunt would like to attend?' Sheward said: 'I am sure she cannot.' The young niece had to be satisfied with that and it appears most of her family did not consider Martha dead, but that she had simply disappeared into the anonymous morass of one of the big cities, probably London. Even when one of Martha's aunts, Mrs Fisher, died and left her some money, Martha's twin sister's husband, Mr Bunn, communicated with Sheward in the hopes of making arrangements. Sheward replied in writing:

I am very sorry to hear of Mrs Fisher's death. At this present I shall not take part in arranging her affairs; therefore you need not expect me, or send me any more about it.

(signed) William Sheward

The Key and Castle public house on Oak Street in the 1930s.

This letter was lodged with Mr Cann, the Wymondham solicitor handling the will of Mrs Fisher.

Sheward was clearly confident he had got away with his crime. He moved away from Tabernacle Street and rented rooms from Mr Bird at St George's. A woman was seen to visit him, and a few months later another woman, who was to become his second wife, was discovered visiting him in June 1852 (almost twelve months to the day after the murder of his wife). The couple were found by the landlord and lady 'in such circumstances as made them feel that if the purity of their house was to be preserved it was necessary to give Sheward notice to quit.' So Sheward and his new paramour, Charlotte Maria Buck, went to live as husband and wife at the Shakespeare pub in St George's. Sheward soon began another pawnbroker business and moved in with his 'wife' above the shop in Lower King Street, near St Peter par Mountergate. The couple lost no time starting a family, Charlotte bearing William four children over the next few years. Sheward and Buck eventually married on 13 February 1862. Sheward described his status on the marriage certificate as 'widower'.

In 1868 Sheward sold his business and stock to his rival, William Boston, pawnbroker of Orford Hill. (It's curious how stories become embroidered – when the fittings and contents of Boston's pawnbrokers were moved to and re-erected in the Bridewell Museum, I was told the murder had actually been committed on the old pawnbroker shop counter, when Sheward stabbed his wife with a pair of scissors!) Sheward's new business venture saw him become the landlord of the dingy Key & Castle pub at 105 Oak Street. This was another bad decision. Sheward may have evaded legal prosecution for his murderous crime, but his conscience would not rest. He rarely had a full night's sleep: people noticed him through the windows, pacing back and forth with a flickering candle in hand. And when cutting a roast joint of meat, a distinct and apparently uncontrollable tremble afflicted his hands. To calm his nerves Sheward started drinking; some even say he was a 'complete alcoholic' by the end of 1868.

Clearly the murder of his wife weighed more heavily on his conscience as each month passed and as more and more drink passed his lips. The Christmas season and the prospect of another New Year of yet more nightmares became intolerable for Sheward and he decided to end it all. Let it not be said he did not have a sense of place and fate akin to that of a Thomas Hardy novel. Sheward resolved to return to the very house on Richmond Street in Walworth, where he had first met the wife he murdered almost eighteen years previously.

Instead of a dramatic act on the doorstep of the house Sheward ended up walking into Carter Street police station, Walworth at 10.30pm on Friday 1 January 1869. Inspector James Davies, an officer of 22 years service on the Metropolitan Police was on duty.

He still thought Sheward might just be overreacting to a violent quarrel or acting under a delusion and tried to get Sheward to think again about what he was saying, but Sheward was quite resolute.

Inspector Davies returned to Sheward in the morning; during the night Sheward had been heard moaning and sobbing on several occasions.

Davies asked Sheward, 'Do you recollect what you said last night?' to which Sheward replied,

'Yes, perfectly well.'

Davies pressed for details of how and when he had committed the crime. Sheward gave the date of the murder as 15 June 1851.

'How was that? How was it the body was not discovered?'

And it was then Sheward confessed he had cut her throat with a razor then cut the body up, and even went so far as to say a portion of it was found and preserved in the Guildhall.

He concluded, 'You will find it quite true; they know all about it at Norwich', but when asked how or when the body was found Sheward said, 'Don't ask me; it's too horrible to talk about.'

After a night in the cells and the dictation of his first confession, Sheward was brought before Lambeth Street Police Court, presided over by Mr Woolrych the Magistrate, and having been remanded in custody, removed to Horsemonger Lane Gaol in London. Inspector Davies then wrote to the Norwich Chief Constable to see if he could ascertain any truth in Sheward's statements. A letter was sent almost by return, confirming that portions of a female body had been found in the city in 1851, and reassuring Davies that 'there is no doubt about the truth of Sheward's statement'. Sheward made his second appearance before the magistrates on 7 January 1869. The confirmation from Norwich was read out and the Magistrate granted the formal application for Sheward to be returned to Norwich to face trial there.

Later on the same day as this hearing, Inspector Davies screwed on the handcuffs – one on Sheward and the other on himself – and escorted his prisoner to Norwich by train. At Trowse, rather than Norwich Thorpe station where a crowd had gathered, Sheward was handed into the custody of Norwich Chief Constable, Robert Hitchman, who took Sheward directly to the Norwich Police Station in a shuttered and anonymous cab – use of the 'Black Maria' police wagon would also have drawn too much attention.

Sheward was brought up on trial at the Norfolk Lent Assizes at the Shirehall on Monday 29 March 1869: an ironic day of judgement, for this day would have been Martha Sheward's seventy-second birthday. In the meantime, the bones of the body parts – buried in what had now become the coal cellar of the Guildhall – were exhumed. The exhumation was witnessed by the ex-butcher Police Sergeant, Edward Peck (by then an inspector), Chief Constable Hitchman, Mr Stanley (Sheward's defence counsel), and Messrs Dalrymple and Nichols – two of the surgeons who had originally examined the body parts. At the previous magisterial hearings Sheward, undoubtedly on the advice of friends and his defence counsel, withdrew the confessional statement he had dictated at Walworth.

The case was brought before Mr Baron Pigott. Mr O'Mally QC led the prosecution and Mr Simms Reeve acted for the defence. As Sheward was brought into the dock between two burly warders he made a pathetic sight. Although just fifty-seven, he was shorter than average, insubstantially built, prematurely aged, and weakened – almost crippled – by the rheumatism

Norwich City Gaol. This whole site is now occupied by the Roman Catholic Cathedral.

he suffered in both ankles. The crowd that packed the public gallery could hardly believe this little old man could have committed such an abominable crime. The case was presented over two days. At 3.05pm on the Tuesday, the jury retired to their deliberations and returned at 4.20pm. The court fell into 'a breathless silence' in anticipation of the verdict. The foreman gravely announced they had found Sheward guilty. Asked if he had any statement to make, Sheward replied faintly: 'I have nothing to say.' Sentence of death was solemnly handed down upon him, and Sheward was removed to Norwich City Gaol (a site now occupied by the Roman Catholic Cathedral). Sheward's rheumatism saw him committed to the gaol infirmary rather than the usual condemned cell. But he wrote his final confession in the condemned cell on 15 April. He also wrote a final letter of thanks to his solicitor, and a long letter thanking his wife for her forgiveness for the pain and shame he had brought to her. He expressed especial gratitude to her for bringing peace to his tortured mind, concluding this, his final letter:

> May the Lords blessing ever attend you and may you and the Children ever be happy is my utmost wish now by God's will I must now bow my head in peace and say goodbye.
> Goodbye
> From Your Unfortunate Husband
> William Sheward

The last execution at Norwich City Gaol, that of Stratford the poisoner, had taken place some forty years previously. Stratford was executed within full view of the public, but due to new national laws, Sheward was to be the first to be executed 'within the prison walls', with no public viewing save a few invited members of the press. Preliminaries for the execution were dealt with by Prison Governor John Howarth. He ordered the scaffold erected at the extreme end of the south-east angle of the prison by Mr Foyson, who also supplied the 'drop' used for executions at the County Gaol at Norwich Castle.

The final date was set for Sheward's execution – 20 April 1869. After spending the previous night at an inn on St Giles Street, Calcraft the Executioner arrived at 5.30am to set up the rope and test the gallows, ready for the appointed hour of execution at 8am. About the same time Sheward awoke. It was noted that – considering it was the night before his execution – Sheward had slept remarkably well. He rose, washed and dressed himself, and declining any last meal, engaged in deep prayer, ready to meet his fate. He was visited by Robert Wade, the Prison Chaplain, between the hours of six and seven, and Wade remained with him from 7.45am, when the prison bell began to toll. Escorted to the Governor's House by Mr Hall, the Chief Warder, Sheward was joined by the Under Sheriff and the Prison Surgeon. After this short walk the combination of fear and the agonising rheumatism he suffered caused Sheward's legs to give way, and Chief Warder Hall and Warder Base had to link hands and carry him to the pinioning room. Remaining fairly composed during the application of the restraints, when about to move off again he was seen to 'shudder with a tremor which was visible throughout his entire frame which never forsook him until life had ceased.'

Sheward was carried to the scaffold, where the Governor and Executioner Calcraft shook his pinioned hands.

William Calcraft, Britain's longest serving public hangman.

The last moments of William Sheward on the scaffold of Norwich City Gaol.

Then Sheward went into earnest prayer until the cap and noose were applied, and when the bolt of the gallows trap was withdrawn, 'the unfortunate man fell, and a slight and brief struggle brought his life to a close.'

Some 2,000 people were waiting in front of the prison gates to see the black flag raised in signal of the completion of the execution. Sheward was buried a short distance from the scaffold, his only grave marker being his initials carved on a stone and set in the wall of the prison by Mr Hibbert, the stonemason of Chapel Field.

4

THE LAST JUDICIAL BEHEADING IN ENGLAND

Walsoken 1885

In the annals of crime and punishment it is rare that the execution of the criminal becomes more infamous than the crime itself, but without doubt, this was the case with Robert Goodale, the Walsoken murderer. His execution at Norwich Castle Gaol not only shocked all those who observed it, but it cast a shadow over the career of James Berry the Public Executioner, and lurked as a fear in the minds of every hangman who came after him.

Our story begins just over the border of Norfolk in Cambridgeshire, at Walsoken Marsh near Wisbech. In this remote area of fenland close to the River Nene, hard-labouring 45-year-old market gardener Robert Goodale, a thickset and powerful man – 'a true son of the soil' – worked a small plot of land. He grew fruit and vegetables and kept a few cattle with Bathsheba, his wife of some twenty-two years, and their sons aged twenty-one and eighteen. Bathsheba owned a number of properties in Wisbech: one where she lived with Robert and the boys, and another occupied by Sarah Ann Goodale, Robert's sister-in-law. She also owned a cottage beside the land they cultivated: consisting of two or three rooms with a well for water outside the back door, this property was thought by Bathsheba to be too remote to live in, so they used it solely for storing fruit. The family set off from Wisbech at eight in the morning to work their land on the marsh until about 6pm, when they would return to sleep at their town house in the evening.

Life was far from a rural idyll. Robert often took to drinking, which led to arguments with Bathsheba – frequently about what he perceived as her bad cooking. She would retort with complaints about Robert's drinking or she accused him of laziness. Over the past six months the rows had become more frequent. Robert had started drinking over longer periods and had been overheard issuing threats of 'I'll knock you down!' when his temper was aggravated by alcohol. Sarah Ann Goodale lived opposite her brother-in-law in Wisbech, and Bathsheba frequently went to her house to avoid

Robert's temper, and shedding many tears, complained how 'tiresome and troublesome' he had become. Over the month preceding September 1885 the arguments and abuse accelerated. Robert would take the cows down to the clover ground in the afternoons and start drinking. Fuelled by strong beer and cider, he would return to the storehouse or garden, seek out Bathsheba, and pick an argument. On one of these occasions George Gage, the farm boy, saw Goodale chase his wife with a hedge hook shouting: 'I'll chop you down if you don't come back!' Bathsheba was terrified and fled in tears to the nearby cottage of the Kierman family. Robert pursued her to the door and knocked upon it. Mrs Harriet Kierman answered. Robert said he did not want to hurt his wife, he just wanted her to come home. Mrs Kierman relayed the message by calling up to Bathsheba. Mrs Goodale replied: 'I will not go, he will kill me.' On another occasion around this time, Mrs Goodale was too frightened to stay in her home with Robert, who was in 'one of his moods', and she went to stay the night with another Wisbech neighbour, Mrs Burton.

Tuesday 15 September 1885 began much as any other day in the Goodale household. They travelled to their plot on Walsoken Marsh and busied themselves during the morning, harvesting the last of their fruit crop and lifting a few potatoes. In the afternoon Robert took the cows down to the

"If you don't come back I'll chop you down."

One of Robert Goodale's drunken threats to his wife.

field. Bob Peck was walking along the riverbank near the storehouse between three and four in the afternoon, and could clearly hear 'two people at high words. One voice was that of a man and the other that of a woman.' Passing again some twenty minutes later he saw Robert and Bathsheba standing close together in the driveway. Robert was seen to walk away from Bathsheba and sit on the bank; she remained where she was. Peck hailed Robert with: 'Nice day!' In a reply tinged with irony Robert answered: 'Yes, it is.' At 4pm Frank Kierman (the nine-year-old son of the Goodales' nearest neighbour to their smallholding) passed by the embankment. Robert was lying down, Bathsheba was sitting near him, and she said to the boy: 'I'll give you some pears if you stop.' Frank said his father had whistled for him to go home and he had better not stop. Frank was the last witness to speak to Mrs Goodale.

Robert Goodale was next seen by Sam Hunt, who spotted him about 100yds from his house. Goodale was alone. It was low water at the time and Hunt judged Goodale to be about 9 or 10ft from the water: his trousers were wet up to the knees, there was what appeared to be mud on his sleeves, and he was engaged in wiping his boots by drawing them along the grass. Hunt called: 'Hello Robert, have you been in the river?' To which he replied: 'I should like to go – shouldn't you?' Hunt passed on with a wave of the hand, not thinking anything untoward had happened.

Tom Spraggins was next to pass, while driving his railway dray to Wisbech at about 5pm. Goodale hailed him: 'Hello young fellow – give us a ride.' Spraggins saw that Goodale's trousers were wet as he scrambled aboard. Spraggins asked how Goodale was getting on with his fruit pulling. He replied, somewhat morosely: 'I think I have pulled all the fruit I shall ever pull,' but quickly added, 'except an odd basket or two for the house.' Spraggins made a delivery at the home of James Walker. This man also knew Goodale and seeing his wet trousers chimed up: 'Hello Robert, have you been fishing?' 'No,' Goodale answered, not rising to any humour. 'I have only been washing myself in the river.' They drove on and Spraggins dropped Goodale at Clarkson's Inn, while he conducted some more business. Returning later, Spraggins collected Goodale and gave him a lift back to Wisbech.

Goodale returned home for the evening, but the boys were soon asking after their mother. Robert said he had left her at the farm. Concerned, the boys went to ask the neighbours if they had seen their mother, but drawing blanks, set off to look for her back at their plot, leaving the impassive Goodale in his chair.

Goulder Gray, a brewer and publican by trade, lived only 10yds from the Goodales' Wisbech home. He was a friend of the family, and having heard Bathsheba was missing, went to see Robert at about 7pm. Gray had noticed the increasing frequency of arguments between Robert and Bathsheba. Gray said: 'There is something said about your wife being absent. Do you know anything about her? She has not returned from the field.' Goodale, almost mumbling, replied: 'I don't know anything about her. I left her there all right.' Sensing Goodale did not want company, Gray left. But as the hours passed, and the boys returned without their mother, concern deepened. Gray returned to the Goodale residence and pressed the same question, expressing a deeper anxiety. Goodale replied: 'I know nothing about her; she has often left me; she'll turn up all right.' Gray said: 'It's very strange that you should sit here in this unconcerned way. Why don't you go and seek for her? If you were a man you would not sit here in this unconcerned way.' When the boys had returned they said the chain was off the well cistern. Gray challenged Goodale about this, who replied: 'There is no cistern; it's blocked up.' Gray added: 'But there is no chain to the well.' Goodale said: 'Yes, I had it to draw some water for the stock this morning and left it there.' The chances are that Gray and a few others had their suspicions aroused by Goodale's behaviour. Gray bravely confronted his neighbour: 'Have you and your wife had any words today?' Goodale replied in a matter-of-fact tone: 'No, we have been more comfortable today than usual.' Gray stayed with Goodale until about 10.30pm and then went home. There was still no sign of Bathsheba. Gray swore Goodale appeared sober.

About 6am on Wednesday the 16th, Gray came down to find Goodale sitting in his taproom, unshaven, and still in his clothes from the night before. Gray asked if Goodale had heard anything more: 'No,' was the blunt reply. Gray reiterated how concerned he was, and how surprised he felt that Robert was so unconcerned: 'Robert, it's your place to search for her.' Goodale got up and left without saying a word. A short while later Goodale was near the sluice and encountered his old pal Joe Barnes, a labourer, who had seen him coming from Gray's house. Goodale looked pale and drawn. He spoke with a tone of resignation: 'I've done the ——— job at last.' Joe, somewhat bemused, asked: 'What job?' To which Goodale replied: 'I've settled her, she won't bark at me any more.' Joe could see his pal was not himself: 'Have some beer,' he proffered. Goodale said he did not have time. He gave Joe 2d to 'get some beer in' and went on his way to Walsoken. Joe had heard nothing of the missing Bathsheba, and judging by the way Goodale looked and spoke, assumed he must have put down his bitch dog. (It must be noted that, at Goodale's trial, the defence counsel presented evidence against this alleged conversation with Barnes, which was tantamount to a confession, by pointing out that Barnes was a previously convicted criminal, and asserting that Barnes had made this statement in an effort to curry favour with the police.)

The previous evening, at about 6pm, Gage the farm boy had drawn water from the well for the horses. The lid was on as usual but he noticed the chain was missing, and upon inspection the normally crystal clear water appeared 'blackified'. Unperturbed he went about his task and returned to Wisbech with one of the Goodale sons. Come the morning, deep concern had seized the friends, neighbours and family of Bathsheba – that is all except her husband

Robert. Renewing their search in the morning, the Goodale sons roped in the help of neighbour William Tooke. With one of the sons Mr Tooke lifted the lid on the well and saw something that disconcerted him enough to get a pole. Inserting the pole down the well, Tooke felt the tip glance something solid – something that bobbed a little when pressed down. Fearing the worst, he got a muck crome, hooked it around part of the object, and pulled it towards the surface. The sight of what arose from the murky, tainted water would haunt Mr Tooke and the Goodale boy for the rest of their lives: it was the battered body of Bathsheba Goodale. The police were sent for and a further search of the farm produced a damp ladder with a bloodstained handprint on top. This was assumed to be the device used to push the body to the bottom of the well.

Police Sergeant Roughton was on the scene about 7.30am, when he saw Goodale on the riverbank. Goodale had been informed that the body of his wife had been found and was gazing into the distance. Roughton approached with caution. He noticed spots of what he thought was blood on Goodale's hat, waistcoat, trousers, and even on his boots. Asked to account for the bloodstains, Goodale said he had had a nosebleed. Roughton announced

The recovery of Bathsheba Goodale's body from the well.

53

he would be taking Goodale into custody on the charge of murdering his wife. Goodale simply replied: 'It's a rum job.' Goodale asked where they had found her and requested that he be taken to see her. Roughton agreed and took Goodale to the uncovered well – quite a crowd had gathered. Roughton and Goodale looked in and saw the grim sight of Bathsheba's pale face, her dead eyes staring accusingly from beneath the surface of the water. Another neighbour, Mr Freeman, got a ladder and a rope, descended the well, placed the rope around the body, and drew it up. The body showed severe wounds to the head. Bathsheba's dress was badly torn and her ulster (a type of double-breasted and belted overcoat) torn in half. On the 17th the well was drained of water and the other half of the ulster, plus a straw hat and glove were found.

It was two months before Robert Goodale was brought before the County Assizes in Norfolk, presided over by Mr Justice Stephen (Sir James Fitzjames Stephen) on Friday 13 November 1885. Although a big man, the weight of the charges brought against him, and his reaction to life in prison, had clearly taken their toll on Goodale. He appeared in the dock a pale and sickly man, a mere shadow of his former self. The witnesses gave their statements and the doctors presented the medical evidence. Mr William Groom, the Wisbech Surgeon, stated he had initially examined the body of Mrs Goodale at the house they used as a store in Walsoken. After relating his initial assessments he expanded on the details relating to the three wounds delivered to her head. After removal of the body and conducting the post-mortem examination, his conclusion was that the wounds had been caused by 'an ordinary billhook'. None of them had proved fatal but rendered her insensible: Bathsheba actually died of drowning. Dr Thomas Stevenson was called and reported on the alleged bloodstains found on Goodale. He could only say some were mammalian. Although there were rust and paint stains on the trousers, which he pointed out could be easily mistaken for blood, no blood was detected on the trousers; but noting the trouser bottoms stiffened by washing, he did add: 'Pure water washed away fresh blood better than anything.'

Throughout the trial Goodale appeared indifferent to the proceedings. Only once did he appear to evince any interest, when a police officer produced the straw hat Bathsheba had been wearing when she was attacked, and it was shown how the cuts in the hat corresponded with the cuts on the dead woman's head. At this point Goodale leaned forward and 'eagerly scrutinised the headgear', after which he relapsed into his former disinterested condition.

After Mr Horace Brown the defence counsel delivered his summing-up to the jury, the Judge, conscious that the hour was getting late, adjourned to the following day, and the jury was retired to special quarters in the Bell Hotel. The following day, Saturday the 14th, the court resumed at 10am sharp. Brown completed his summing-up and Mr Blofield presented his summary for the prosecution. After a balanced summing-up by Judge Stephen the jury retired at 1.30pm and returned just fifteen minutes later to present a verdict of 'Guilty'. The Clerk of Arraigns asked Goodale if he had anything to say, and according to an eyewitness, Goodale 'apparently made an effort to speak, but no sound escaped his lips.' The Judge assumed the black cap and the dread sentence was passed:

> This court doth ordain that you, Robert Goodale, be taken to the place from whence you came and from thence to a place of execution, and there you be hung by the neck until you be dead and that after your execution your body be buried in the prison in which you shall have been then last before your execution, and may the Lord have mercy on you soul.

Goodale was seen to grip the dock rail firmly as sentence was passed. He appeared to want to speak but no words came and he was removed immediately after to the cells. The date set for his execution was Monday 30 November 1885.

A little-known fact is that the duty of carrying out a death sentence is not the responsibility of the police, prison or judiciary, as most people may expect. The responsibility of engaging and paying for an executioner falls to the Acting or Under-Sheriff of the county in which the sentence is passed. The reason for this apparent anomaly has ancient roots, but by the nineteenth and twentieth centuries the Under-Sheriff dealt with such matters because he was 'a person who had no official position under the Government and no motive for condoning any irregularity'. If the law had been followed to the letter, Under-Sheriffs would have carried out executions too, but they were free to appoint a stand-in. Some appointed their own private executioners, but most consulted a Home Office list of approved executioners, upon whose services they could call.

The Norfolk Under-Sheriff, Mr J.B.T. Hales was no doubt confident when he secured the services of James Berry, the country's Chief Executioner. Berry was a strongly built, no-nonsense Yorkshireman. Coming from Bradford, Berry had previously been employed in a variety of jobs, including a railway porter, shoe salesman and even a police constable, but had found his métier as Public Executioner. An efficient and methodical man in his work as executioner, he was equally adept in his business practice, and was the first executioner to issue ready-made printed invoices. These clearly laid out his terms of employment: £10 for carrying out the execution, £5 if the condemned was reprieved plus travelling expenses.

Unfortunately, 1885 had not been a good year for Executioner Berry. On 23 February he was at Exeter to carry out the execution of John Lee for the murder of his employer at Babbacombe near Torquay. Lee swore his

At the delivery of the Gaols of our Lady the Queen of the
Winter Assize County N.º 7
holden at the Castle of Norwich in the County of Norfolk
in and for the said Winter Assize County on
the Ninth day of November in the forty ninth Year
of the Reign of our Sovereign Lady Queen Victoria, and in
the Year of our Lord 1885 Before The Honourable
Sir James Fitzjames Stephen, Knight,
one of the Justices of the High Court of
Justice.

and others their fellows, Justices of our said Lady the Queen,
assigned to deliver the aforesaid Gaols of the prisoners therein
being.

Robert Goodale. Is convicted of Murder, and it is
ordered and adjudged that he be taken from
hence to the place from whence he came,
and from thence to a place of lawful
Execution, and that he be there hanged by
the neck until he be dead, and that his body
be afterwards buried within the precincts of the
Prison in which he shall have been last
confined after this his conviction

Platt.
Clerk of Assize

The death warrant for Robert Goodale. (*Norfolk Record Office*)

Executioner Berry's
pro forma invoice, for
services rendered.

> QUOTE
> No.
>
> *Bradford,* 189
> YORKS.
>
> Sir,
>
>   I beg leave to state in reply to your letter
> of the .... that I
> am prepared to undertake the execution you name of
>
> _____
>
> at .... on the ....
>
>   I also beg leave to state that my terms are as
> follows: £10 for the execution, £5 if the condemned
> is reprieved, together with all travelling expenses.
>   Awaiting your reply,
>   I am, Sir,
>   Your obedient Servant,
>
>   James Berry.
>
> The High Sheriff,
>   for the County of ....

innocence and had a dream the night before that he would not hang for the crime. In what has become arguably the most folklore-ridden of British executions, Lee was made ready and placed on the gallows trap, the noose around his neck, the lever was pushed – but the trap refused to open. Lee was removed and the trap tested: it fell open easily. Set closed again, Lee was put on the drop and the lever was pushed: but still it would not open, despite Berry and the warders adding their weight by stamping on the trapdoors. Lee was removed from the chamber and the trap tested again – and it worked with no problems. A third time Lee was brought back, made ready to meet his maker, but the trapdoors failed yet again. The Chaplain appealed to the Governor to intercede, but it was the medical officer who stepped forward and said to Berry: 'You may experiment as much as you like on a sack of flour, but you shall not experiment on this man any longer.' Lee was granted a reprieve from death but had to serve a life sentence.

Berry recovered his nerve to carry out the next couple of executions, but then there was Moses Shrimpton, a 65-year-old poacher who had killed a police officer. Berry worked out the 'drop' from the prescribed table, but had not considered the weakness of the old man's neck and almost tore Shrimpton's head from his body. Although there was no criticism as such at the inquest that followed, Berry was no doubt alarmed. But Berry regained his confidence over his next six 'drops', performed in the execution chambers of various prisons. Berry initially supplied ropes that conformed to his own specifications: made from Italian hemp ¾in thick, 13ft long, and with the

James Berry, the
executioner,
c. 1885.

SCALE SHOWING THE STRIKING FORCE OF FALLING BODIES AT DIFFERENT DISTANCES.

Distance Falling in Feet	8 Stone	9 Stone	10 Stone	11 Stone	12 Stone	13 Stone	14 Stone	15 Stone	16 Stone	17 Stone	18 Stone	19 Stone
Zero	Cw. Qr. lb.	Cw. Qr. lb.	Cw. Qr. lb.	Cw. Qr. lb.	Cw. Qr. lb.	Cw. Qr. lb.	Cw. Qr. lb.	Cw. Qr. lb.	Cw. Qr. lb.	Cw. Qr. lb.	Cw. Qr. lb.	Cw. Qr. lb.
1 Ft.	8 0 0	9 0 0	10 0 0	11 0 0	12 0 0	13 0 0	14 0 0	15 0 0	16 0 0	17 0 0	18 0 0	19 0 0
2 ,,	11 1 15	12 2 23	14 0 14	15 2 4	16 3 22	18 1 12	19 3 2	21 0 21	22 2 11	24 0 1	25 1 19	26 3 9
3 ,,	13 3 16	15 2 15	17 1 14	19 0 12	20 3 11	22 2 9	24 1 8	26 0 7	27 3 5	29 2 4	31 1 2	33 0 1
4 ,,	16 0 0	18 0 0	20 0 0	22 0 0	24 0 0	26 0 0	28 0 0	30 0 0	32 0 0	34 0 0	36 0 0	40 0 0
5 ,,	17 2 11	19 3 5	22 0 0	24 0 22	26 1 16	28 2 11	30 3 5	33 0 0	35 0 22	37 0 16	39 2 11	41 3 15
6 ,,	19 2 11	22 0 5	24 2 0	26 3 22	29 1 16	31 3 11	34 1 5	36 3 0	39 0 22	41 2 16	44 0 11	46 2 5
7 ,,	21 0 22	23 3 11	26 2 0	29 0 16	31 3 5	34 1 22	37 0 11	39 3 0	42 1 16	45 0 5	47 2 22	50 1 11
8 ,,	22 2 22	25 2 4	28 1 14	31 0 23	34 0 5	36 3 15	39 2 25	42 2 7	45 1 16	48 0 26	51 0 8	53 3 18
9 ,,	24 0 11	27 0 12	30 0 14	33 0 23	36 0 16	39 0 18	42 0 19	45 0 21	48 0 22	51 0 23	54 0 25	57 0 26
10 ,,	25 1 5	28 1 23	31 2 14	34 3 4	37 3 22	41 0 12	44 1 2	47 1 21	50 2 11	53 3 1	56 3 19	60 0 9

The table of drops to aid the calculations of the executioner.

noose formed by the rope running through a brass ring spliced into one end (not the typical rope with 'hangman's knot' commonly used in America and so often depicted in films). Keen to standardise and assure quality, modern governments preferred to issue operatives with their essential equipment, rather than allow them to use their own, and this included hangman's ropes (this was also an attempt to stop the sale of grim relics, such as lengths of hangman's rope). Although made to a similar specification to his own, the rope Berry was to use for Goodale was supplied by the Government. And as Berry liked to use 'tried and tested' ropes at executions, he brought along the one he had used the previous week on John Williams at Hereford.

Berry arrived at Norwich Castle Gaol and took up his quarters on the afternoon of Saturday 28 November, leaving him time to attend divine service and have the rest of the day clear to ensure all the preparations were made for the execution on Monday morning.

Goodale's conduct in prison was exemplary. He was granted attendance by a Baptist minister, the Revd T.A. Wheeler. His sister and two sons bade him a final visit on Friday the 27th, and on the same evening Goodale requested to speak with the Prison Governor, Mr A.E. Dent, who immediately went to the condemned cell with the Chief Warder. Goodale stated he wished to unburden his mind and confessed he had struck his wife as a result of her saying she liked other men better than him. He claimed he had 'struck her down with a piece of iron which laid on the ground near him', pleading extreme provocation. Goodale further claimed that his wife fell down the well after being struck, and that he did not push her. He maintained that he used the bloodstained ladder in an attempt to rescue her, not to push her down. Despite medical evidence to the contrary, and witness statements confirming the long history of arguments, threats and violence between Goodale and his wife, the Governor forwarded Goodale's 'confession' to the Home Secretary and communicated these latest developments to Revd Wheeler. As a result, Wheeler and Mr W.H. Dakin, the ex-Sheriff of Norwich, proceeded to London for an interview with the Under-Secretary of State. Neither application availed any reprieve for Goodale.

Berry was informed that Goodale was a big man, weighing 15 stone and measuring 5ft 11ins in height. He was the second largest man Berry had executed. According to the Marwood's 'Table of Drops', Goodale would require a drop of 7ft 8ins (William Marwood was the previous Chief Executioner, who compiled a table that helped executioners to calculate the length of rope or 'drop' necessary to break the condemned's neck – if the 'drop' was too short it could lead to strangulation; if too long it could result in damage to the neck), but Berry was not happy with this length. Berry had met Goodale in his cell but did not reveal his identity. It was plain to see that Goodale was a physical wreck, and despite being a big-framed man, his neck was 'not very muscular': so Berry shortened the drop to 5ft 9in. The Surgeon asked Berry if he thought this was enough of a drop to avoid strangulation; Berry assured him it would be enough. The Governor was particularly anxious about the whole affair. He had erected the scaffold to Home Office specifications, and one man had already been executed on it, but the Governor remained uneasy. He apparently insisted on testing the drop on the Thursday before the execution, and again on the Saturday before Berry arrived, this time in the presence of the prison engineer.

The officials for the execution – Under-Sheriff J.B.T. Hales, Mr Haynes S. Robinson the Gaol Surgeon, Governor Dent and an invited number of local press men – gathered at the prison from an early hour on 30 November 1885. At 7.30am on the morning of the execution Berry conducted his final tests on the gallows in the presence of the Under-Sheriff, using a 16-stone weight, as recommended by Home Office regulations. All seemed satisfied that everything had been done 'by the book' and with proper consideration to ensure the execution went smoothly. Goodale had slept soundly over Sunday night. Waking at 5am, he asked for something to eat almost as soon as his cell door was opened. Revd Wheeler also attended Goodale during his last hours in the condemned cell.

At 7.55am the great bell of St Peter Mancroft Church began to toll, and the officials gathered by the condemned cell to make their dread procession to the prison bathroom, where Goodale would be pinioned. Berry recalled that the screams and cries of Goodale echoed around the prison. His fellow inmates shouted and beat on their doors in reply. Goodale had to be led down the passage to where he was to be pinioned, and according to Berry:

> When I went forward to pinion him he was crying like a little child. Approaching him from behind I slipped the strap around his body. He wriggled to prevent me buckling it, and I had to tell him in a firm tone to be a man.

Eventually securing the pinions, it was time to move off on the final walk to the gallows. Goodale refused to move and had to be dragged along, screaming and shouting. The gathered officials – and indeed Berry – were unnerved by Goodale's display.

As Goodale got closer to the gallows he was seen to break down physically and mentally, seeming to pass between a state of collapse and terror in which he repeated, 'Oh, God, receive my soul' a number of times. When in position on the trap it appeared that Goodale's legs would not support him any longer, so two warders were positioned beside him to hold him up, while Berry put the final pinion around his legs, the white bag over his head, and adjusted the noose around his neck. Berry, with the fatal lever in hand, asked Goodale: 'Do you wish to say anything?' Goodale replied in the negative and before the church bells of Norwich struck the final chime of eight Berry pulled the lever, the traps fell open, and Goodale was shot to eternity. Berry recorded what happened next in his memoirs: 'We were horrified, however, to see the rope jerked upwards and for an instant I thought the noose had slipped from the culprit's head or that the rope had broken.'

As the black flag was hoisted over the right-hand entrance to the Gaol, informing the crowd outside that the execution had been carried out, the Governor, the Gaol Surgeon and Berry looked into the pit below. Berry continues, having feared the noose had slipped off Goodale's head:

> it was worse than that for the jerk had severed the head entirely from the body and both had fallen into the bottom of the pit. Of course death was instantaneous so that the poor fellow had not suffered in any way; but it was terrible to think such a revolting thing should have occurred. We were all unnerved and shocked. The Governor, whose efforts to prevent any accident had kept his nerves at full strain, fairly broke down and wept.

When the onlookers had recovered their composure an inquest was held on the body of Robert Goodale (as demanded by Home Office regulations) in the Magistrates' Room at the Castle, presided over by the Coroner, E.S. Bignold, Esq. The witnesses all spoke favourably of Berry's thoroughness: pointing out, when asked, that the Executioner was sober. Goodale's head had been severed

The imaginative rendition of the end of Robert Goodale from the *Illustrated Police News*.

from the body as cleanly as if cut by a knife. The jury considered the evidence and their views were clear: 'Robert Goodale came to his death by hanging according to judgement of law, and in answer to the Coroner, the jury did not consider anyone was to blame for what had occurred.'

Although acquitted of any blame, the 'Goodale Mess' haunted Berry for the rest of his career and probably for the rest of his life. Berry executed a total of 131 condemned criminals, both men and women, in a career spanning seven years. In 1892 he retired, and after a brief lecture tour, found religion. Berry 'gave himself to Jesus' and began visiting evangelical churches as a preacher. Charles Mackie, author of the Norfolk historian's essential *Norfolk Annals*, had been present at the execution as a reporter on the *Norfolk Chronicle*. He recalled the execution when surveying his career many years later. With some pride he declared he had been present at what could justifiably be called 'the last judicial beheading in England'.

5

THE SOUTH BEACH MURDERS

Great Yarmouth 1900 and 1912

At about 6.10am on Sunday 23 September 1900, fourteen-year-old John Norton set out from his home at 36 Boreham Road, Great Yarmouth, for another day on the beach at Hewitt's Hut, where he worked during the bathing season. Norton walked along the track used for carting purposes in a direct line from Barrack Road, between the Barracks and the Naval Hospital. While passing along South Parade, near the telegraph house, Norton looked out to sea across the South Beach and noticed a woman lying, apparently asleep, about 20yds away from the parade, near the south end of the Naval Hospital wall. The area of the South Beach in question is situated between Wellington Pier and the Pleasure Beach. Even today this area of the beach remains undeveloped, with undulating dunes and gullies, liberally sprinkled with outcrops of marram grass. The privacy of these natural hollows after dark made it an area well known to the courting couples of Yarmouth.

When Norton reported for work at the bathing chalet he told his boss, Mr Grief, what he had seen. They both knew that despite the strict council by-laws a few folks would sleep on the beach in the summer if they could not find accommodation, so Mr Grief sent the boy back to wake the woman up before the beach inspector caught her. Young Norton scampered back, no doubt looking forward to seeing the surprised expression on the lady's face when he woke her up. She had not stirred, and as he approached he sensed something was amiss. Getting close, he saw her clothes and hair were spattered with sand. Her eyes were open, her face was badly bruised and scratched, and most horrible of all, some sort of ligature had been drawn so tight around her neck it had burrowed into the skin. She was clearly dead and Norton wasted no time: turning on his heels he ran to look for a policeman.

The first officer encountered by the boy was PC Manship, who was on duty near the Jetty on Marine Parade. Norton related his tale between gasps for breath and led Manship to the body. Reaching the site about 6.30am

Manship committed the scene to memory and wrote it up later in his report. He noted the woman was

lying flat on her back on the sand with her head to the south. Her hands were by her side and fingers bent into the palms. Beneath her was a white pocket-handkerchief and beside her, close to the right side of her head was laying a white straw sailor hat, with a black band around it. To it was attached a black net veil spotted with white (it was later noted that the hat must have been taken off with some care – white-headed hatpins, despite being bent, were intact in the hat, their points going through old and regularly used holes in the straw), her hair was unfastened and was all down her shoulders . . . I then particularly took notice of where she lay, and the sand all round. It appeared there had been a struggle, in one place in particular, about 4yds to the right of the body . . . her skirt was drawn up the right leg a trifle above the knee, and just below the left knee. Her left leg was slightly bent. Her bloomers (later found to be stained with menstrual blood and blood from a small cut) were down to her ankles.

A modern view of the dunes on South Beach.

There was also a tear in the bloomers of about 7 or 8ins long – it was never firmly ascertained if this tear was caused by her assailant. Upon a closer examination of the body the ligature around her neck was found to be a mohair bootlace. Before becoming a policeman Manship had been at sea for seven years. He noted the type of knots tied in the lace: a reef knot at the back of the neck, at which another section of lace had been joined (a mend to the old lace), and two reef knots to the left-front secured with a granny knot on top to prevent slipping.

Having completed his survey of the body and crime scene, PC Manship sent Norton to William Wood of 60 Ordnance Road for a horse and cart to remove the body to the North Quay Mortuary. The following officials were then summoned: Dr Lettis, the Police Surgeon; William Parker, Yarmouth Borough Police Chief Constable; and Sergeant John Moore, the Coroner's Officer. They were joined by detectives from the local police: DI Robert Lingwood and Detectives Platten and Woodruff. The post-mortem was performed by Dr Lettis assisted by Dr O'Farrell.

Within hours news of the grim discovery had spread like wildfire across Great Yarmouth, becoming more and more lurid with each telling. One rumour claimed the woman had been subjected to multiple stab wounds. Another suggested: 'the dead woman had been done to death after the manner of the poor creatures that were murdered by the mysterious Jack the Ripper, and that the body had been shockingly mutilated.'

The police jumped to no immediate conclusions. Murder looked most likely, but they did consider suicide as another option, her wounds having been caused by her death throes. But on closer examination it was found that the knots in the lace could not have been tied and applied by the victim.

Around the same time as the body was being examined at the mortuary, Mrs Eliza Rudrum, landlady of a lodging house at 3 Row 104, mentioned to her husband John her displeasure at finding Mrs Hood's child awake and crying. There was no sign of the mother: she had gone out the previous night after putting the child to bed and had not returned. Mrs Rudrum assumed she had spent a night in a lover's arms. But on hearing news of the murder from neighbour Edward Fish, Eliza wanted to inform the police of her lodger's absence, but her husband dissuaded her, saying it was too soon to consider such a thing.

As it happened, Mr Fish was on his way out to fetch some milk and chanced upon a police constable in Middlegate Street. No doubt hoping to learn the latest on the murder, he stopped for a chat and mentioned the missing lodger in passing. The Constable acted immediately, reporting promptly to the Police Station a little further up Middlegate Street. He was told to fetch John Rudrum and escort him to the mortuary, to see if he could identify the woman. Rudrum informed the police that the missing woman was a Mrs Hood, who in conversation had given her age as twenty-seven. She and her daughter Rose (a child said by Mrs Hood to be one year and eleven months old) had been lodging with the Rudrums since 15 September. On the night in question Mrs Hood had put the child to bed, leaving her in the care of the Rudrums, and had gone out to meet someone.

DI Lingwood proceeded to the Rudrums' lodging house. An initial search of Mrs Hood's room revealed a cheap photograph (a tin-type) 'in a common frame' as used by beach photographers. The photograph, taken on the beach, showed a woman with the little girl he had seen in the lodging house. The woman in the photograph certainly looked like the woman in the mortuary: she was even wearing the same dove grey skirt, embroidered with broad white braid, worked into a scroll design down the side. Mrs Rudrum's husband was taken to view the body and confirmed it was that of the woman who had been staying with them.

There were, however, few other clues – apart from a purse belonging to Mrs Hood, which contained a return ticket to Yarmouth from London and a latchkey, but no money. DI Lingwood questioned Mrs Rudrum for any other information about Mrs Hood. Rudrum could only relate what she had learned in conversation. Mrs Hood had claimed she was a widow who had a home in Yorkshire. She had been anticipating the arrival of a letter from Woolwich, which arrived on Friday the 21st. Mrs Rudrum had seen part of the letter when Mrs Hood left it on the table. She recalled that it read: 'Put your child to bed and meet me at the big clock at nine o'clock' and was signed with the name Hood. Mrs Rudrum's daughter Alice had seen the envelope and noted the Woolwich postmark, but no trace of either the letter or the envelope was ever found by the police. Mrs Hood said her brother-in-law, who was in love with her and was jealous of her, was also staying in Great Yarmouth in one of the hotels 'and she should not be surprised if he was following her about'.

About 10.50 that same night, Alice had seen Mrs Hood with a man on the quay at the end their Row. She could not distinguish any of his features, but heard him say to Mrs Hood: 'You understand don't you, that I am placed in a very awkward position right now?' He then kissed her, bade goodnight, and left. Mrs Hood then returned to her lodgings. On the Saturday, Mrs Hood had spent most of the day getting ready to go out that evening. Once her little girl was put to bed she went out and was seen by Alice on the west side of the town hall facing the river. Alice spoke to Mrs Hood but she did not reveal who she was apparently waiting for. Alice was the last person to see Mrs Hood alive.

On the Sunday, Mr Frank Sayers, a Yarmouth commercial photographer – more used to taking family portraits in studios – was instructed to take photographs of the body in the mortuary, and of the crime scene on the South Beach. Frank recalled the event years later:

I had been often called upon to do strange photographic work but I had never undertaken anything of this sort, and I may say now that the whole

A typical Yarmouth Row, such as the one in which 'Mrs Hood' lodged.

affair knocked the nerve out of me and haunted me like a nightmare for many months.

A fascinating parallel with the Ripper enquiry, which had taken place over ten years before, is the Yarmouth Police's use of the 'French Method' of photographing the retina of the murder victim, in the hope it retained an image of the last person seen – most likely the killer. This method was said to be carried out on at least one of the Ripper's victims but to no effect. The result of this process in the Yarmouth Beach Murder was also unsuccessful, it's failure being attributed 'to the fact that the deceased was done to death while it was dark'.

Meanwhile, police concentrated their immediate enquiries on the Yarmouth hotels, in an attempt to trace Hood's brother-in-law. Attempts were also made to track Mrs Hood's antecedents in Yorkshire and Woolwich, but local police could do little to inform other constabularies that day, because the telegraph office was only open between the hours of five and six on Sunday afternoons. But by Monday evening, photographer Frank Sayers had made copies of the beach photograph, which were despatched on twelve routes across the country, circulating from town to town.

The only other clue police had to go on was a laundry mark found on Mrs Hood's underclothes, bearing the number '599'. This information was also circulated.

The inquest was due to open on 25 September, but as enquiries to ascertain the identity of Mrs Hood or the whereabouts of her relatives were proving inconclusive, it was twice adjourned. The inquest finally took place on the evening of Thursday the 27th, when Coroner J.T. Waters, Esq. opened proceedings at the Town Hall. He pointed out that beyond the information provided by Mrs Rudrum, nothing had been forthcoming to confirm the identity of Mrs Hood. The Coroner also drew the court's attention to the fact that the woman had been wearing knickerbockers, and that they were unbuttoned, declaring this 'an important point'. He also noted the right thigh of the deceased was covered in sand, a fact he thought 'worthy of consideration'. At the inquest the Rudrums retold what they knew of their mysterious lodger and her young child, and John Norton spoke of how he discovered the body.

On the second day of the inquest, proceedings commenced on the afternoon of Friday the 28th. Poor PC Manship, despite giving clear testimony, was criticised by the Coroner for not making notes upon discovering the body, and for removing the body to the mortuary without summoning his senior officer or detectives beforehand. Police Surgeon Lettis and Dr O'Farrell, presenting their findings to the inquest, concluded that the cause of death had been asphyxia caused by the ligature: the way the knots were tied, and the tightness achieved, could not have been done by the victim. They mentioned two or three small bruises, one of which was a laceration to the intimate areas of the woman, suggesting rape had been attempted but not effected. The bruises on her face implied misapplication of the ligature: in haste it was first wound around her chin, tightened, found to be in the wrong place, and then removed to her throat. The scratches on either side of the nose were thought to have been made by the killer placing his hands on the victim's face, with the palms pressing on the jaw at either side and the fingertips injuring the face where the marks were found. It was confirmed that if the lace had been tied quickly, the victim would not have had a chance to scream.

At the same time as the Friday inquest the body of Mrs Hood was enclosed in a redwood coffin – 'of a better quality than that usually provided for those unfortunate enough to be buried on the parish' – and placed on the mortuary's hand ambulance. It was then wheeled via North Quay and Fullers Hill to the parish church by the mortuary keeper, Guardian's undertaker and the boys' caretaker at the workhouse – all in full mourning attire. Many people, notably those from George Street, guessing this was the funeral cortège of the beach murder victim, hurriedly joined in and followed as mourners. Taken to the church and finally the cemetery, by the time the coffin reached the grave, prepared in the North West section, there were about 200 mourners present. Here the final act of committal was led by the curate, Revd H.B. Rivington. Mrs Rudrum and her daughter were at the graveside, as were Inspector Lingwood, Inspector Harrison, and a number of other officers. The lid bore no nameplate but had two metallic shields as ornaments. In the church and cemetery register the deceased was entered as 'The Unknown' with the word Hood in parenthesis. The little girl Rose remained in the care of the Rudrums.

Despite growing national media attention and a final verdict of wilful murder against 'a man unknown', the search for the true identity of 'Mrs Hood' produced no leads. During the second week of October, Yarmouth's Chief Constable, William Parker, made the decision he was not making enough headway with his local team and called in Scotland Yard, who assigned Chief Inspector Alfred Leach of the CID to the case. In early November the break they were all hoping for came when the laundry mark was finally traced to the Bexleyheath Laundry. It transpired that no Mrs Hood was allocated that number: it was Mrs Mary Jane Bennett of 1 Glencoe Villa, Bexleyheath. Further enquiries revealed she had not lived there since mid-September. A tip-off led police to her husband, 21-year-old Herbert John Bennett.

On 8 November Chief Inspector Leach went to Woolwich to interview Bennett. Shown the beach photograph, Bennett claimed he did not recognise either mother or child. When formally arrested Bennett said: 'I don't understand what you mean. I have never been to Yarmouth. I have not been with my wife since January as I found a lot of letters in her pocket from

The photograph that was to be so telling – Mary Bennett and daughter Ruby on Yarmouth Beach.

another man.' When Bennett's lodgings were searched at 18 William Street, police discovered a receipt from the Crown and Anchor Hotel in Yarmouth dated 6 August, a revolver, and curious items such as male and female wigs and a false moustache. More significantly, the police also found a long gold necklace and silver watch, similar to those worn by 'Mrs Hood' in Great Yarmouth and discernible on the beach photograph.

Bennett was brought under arrest to Great Yarmouth. He was remanded at the Police Court and appeared before a Quarter Sessions packed with spectators and reporters on 16 November. On his way to and from court in the black police wagon, crowds lined the streets booing and jeering. From the moment of his arrest the local press had put Bennett squarely in the frame for the crime. Lurid pamphlets of 'scurrilous verses' about 'Bennett the Beach Murderer' caused grave concerns over Bennett receiving a fair trial in Norfolk. An application was made to the King's Bench and granted without much difficulty to remove the trial to the Central Criminal Court – the Old Bailey in London.

By the time of the trial the tangled web of Bennett's past had been unravelled and laid bare by the press. The woman in the photograph and the murder victim was undoubtedly 23-year-old Mary Jane Bennett, the child was indeed hers but she was not called Rose; her name was Ruby. A talented musician, Mary had met Herbert in 1896 when he came to her for music

The grave of 'Mrs Hood'.

The departure of a criminal (possibly Herbert Bennett) from the Great Yarmouth police headquarters on Middlegate Street, *c.* 1900.

lessons as a sixteen-year-old wanting to play violin and piano. They fell in love and wished to marry. Herbert's parents were not keen on their son marrying at such a young age, but when Mary fell pregnant in the spring of 1897 and Herbert wanted to 'make an honest woman of her', the parents had to agree. And so the couple married and went to live with Mary's grandmother in the flat above the family butcher's shop. Tragically, the Bennett's baby was stillborn. Early in 1898 Mary conceived again but their joy was short-lived. Mary's grandmother died leaving almost everything to Mary's father, who promptly gave his daughter and son-in-law immediate notice to quit. The only thing he did not dispute was Mary's right to her grandmother's gold chain.

With but a few trinkets and about £15 the Bennetts went to live at Clapham Junction, where they bought a small dwelling with a lower floor crudely converted for selling green vegetables and coal. On 13 October their baby, Ruby Bennett, was born. The couple were in dire straits and they turned to petty deceptions to earn money: the most lucrative being the purchase of cheap violins, which Mary would advertise in *Bazaar* and *Exchange and Mart*, posing as the poor widow of a professor, doctor or gentleman, who hitting hard times, was forced to sell her late husband's prized violin, case, strings etc. Thing were going well and the Bennetts invested in larger business premises with accommodation above at 5 Station Road, Westgate-on-Sea. This shop suffered a mysterious fire that gutted it. The insurance company paid up and Bennett made a further £107 auctioning off salvaged stock. Staying on another four weeks, the Bennetts filled the gutted shop with goods bought on credit, which they sold at knock-down prices, and did a moonlight flit with the profits, leaving their creditors high and dry.

Then came a mysterious trip to South Africa – attributed by some historians of the case as an attempt to offer themselves as spies for the Boers – but the Bennetts returned after just four days. Their relationship, however, was in decline. Their lodging housekeeper recalled they frequently argued. And so they separated: Herbert lodged in Woolwich at 41 Union Street and Mary went to Bexleyheath, obtaining a residence on a false reference provided by Herbert. He frequently visited Mary and the child there, and neighbours thought nothing amiss with the couple.

After a sojourn with the Royal Arsenal Co-op, Herbert went to work as a labourer at the Royal Arsenal. Through a colleague at the arsenal, Herbert met the pretty 22-year-old parlour maid, Alice Meadows. Herbert was smitten with Alice and he never let on he had a wife and child, covering visits to Mary by claiming he was visiting a sick cousin. Herbert wrote Alice a long stream of love letters and they were 'walking out' together on most of their days off. They went on holiday to Yarmouth for the August Bank Holiday. Bennett was the epitome of propriety: they had separate rooms at the Crown and Anchor Hotel on Hall Quay. A few weeks later they were off on holiday again, this time to Ireland. On the morning of their departure Bennett proposed to Alice and she came back from Ireland sporting a fine ruby and diamond engagement ring.

To those who put the pieces together from both sides of the marriage, the split appeared irreparable between Mary and Herbert Bennett, but then, they were both accomplished liars – could anyone really tell who was scamming who? On Saturday 15 September Herbert told Alice he was visiting his sick grandfather in Gravesend. Mary had told neighbours she was off for a stay in Yarmouth with her husband and child. John Rudrum stated he had seen 'Mrs Hood' turn into the Row with a man on the night of the 15th, but it was a fleeting glimpse and Rudrum could not describe the man. At Bennett's trial others came forward to testify that Bennett was seen at Yarmouth on the night of the murder and the morning after. But as to why Mary had concealed her identity, and who she met in the Row (as witnessed by Alice Rudrum when time sheets show conclusively that Herbert was at work in the arsenal), these questions were never conclusively answered.

Bennett was fortunate enough to obtain the services of one of the most brilliant defence counsels of his age – Edward Marshall Hall. When the brief for defence was delivered, the evidence against Bennett seemed overwhelming – the press had seen to that. And Bennett had not helped himself by showing

Herbert Bennett in the dock at the Old Bailey.

himself as an accomplished liar, who not only made deception a way of life in business, but also in his relationship with the innocent and trusting Alice Meadows. For this reason alone, Bennett would have been viewed as a scoundrel – not to mention the arguments overheard between the Bennetts, when Herbert was heard to say 'he wished she was dead, and that, if she didn't look out, she soon would be', and she countered that she could 'get him fifteen years' (probably for revealing he had committed arson on his own shop to get the insurance money – although it seems he may also have been a blackmailer). Bennett's alibi for the fateful night of Mary's murder (22 September) also proved to be a lie. Upon his arrest Bennett had provided the names of two men, Messrs William Parritt and James Cameron, with whom he said he was drinking at the Prince Albert, Woolwich on the night in question. Both men vehemently denied this. But then a strange thing happened. Marshall Hall interviewed Bennett in his cell at Norwich Prison: he did not like the man and could see he was someone who could not tell the truth, but Marshall Hall was convinced Bennett was not Mary's murderer.

Brought to London from Norwich on 11 February, the trial of Herbert Bennett opened on 25 February 1901: he would have the dubious honour of being the first man to stand on a capital charge at the Old Bailey in the twentieth century. Smartly dressed in dark overcoat and grey suit, looking pale but fit, Bennett did not show any ill effects from his weeks in prison awaiting trial. Marshall Hall knew if the prosecution could bring to bear the accusations voiced in the press the case was lost. Marshall Hall eloquently argued that there was no conclusive proof from any witness to place Bennett in Yarmouth on the night of the murder. The most compelling prosecution testimony could have come from Alfred Mason (aged nineteen) and his girlfriend Blanche Smith (aged seventeen), who were on the South Beach on the night of the murder. They had not been keeping an eye on the time, but noticed a couple who passed nearby, apparently arguing. Alfred noticed the shiny material of the woman's dress and that the man was wearing a dark suit but no hat. When this couple were about 30yds away from Mason and Smith, they were seen to sit down on some sloping ground. All seemed well until Blanche heard the woman groaning and calling for mercy. They assumed the couple were 'larking about' but then all fell silent. After ten minutes of silence, Alfred and Blanche became uneasy. They got up and left the beach, passing within about 5yds of the other couple. It was light enough to see that the woman was lying on her back, with the man crouching or kneeling over her. As they passed the man turned his head and looked full at them. It was too dark to make out his features: consequently, neither of them could identify Bennett.

Marshall Hall incisively tackled the three key prosecution witnesses who placed Bennett at Yarmouth on the night of the murder and on the following morning.

William Reade, a waiter at the Crown and Anchor in Yarmouth, swore Herbert Bennett was the man he saw staying there on the night of the 15th who left early for his train on the 16th. He remembered Bennett from his previous stay with Alice Meadows during the August Bank Holiday, when Reade had attended to them. Reade continued:

Alice Meadows sketched at the time of the trial. *(Great Yarmouth Local Studies Library)*

Hall Quay, Great Yarmouth, *c.* 1900. The Crown and Anchor Hotel, where Bennett allegedly stayed on the night of the murder, is on the left; the Row lodging house where his wife was staying was but a few minutes' walk away.

> I saw him again on 22 September. He asked for a bed . . . He said he wished to have breakfast at 7am. He told me he was down on business when I remarked that it was strange he should leave so early.

Marshall Hall argued in his closing speech for the defence that Reade had only come forward to the police after Bennett's arrest, when the press was full of the story and Bennett's picture had been widely published. Reade was scorned by Marshall Hall for giving his story to the press, which he pronounced as 'utterly unreliable and untrustworthy'.

Mr J.W. Headley, a Great Yarmouth newsagent, was on the station collecting parcels of newspapers at 7am on the 23rd. He recalled a theatrical company leaving that morning and noted the incongruous behaviour of a lone man standing near the first-class carriage, who appeared 'very agitated and excited, looking up and down the platforms in an anxious manner'. In cross-examination Marshall Hall pressed Headley: 'Will you swear this is the man you saw?' To which Headley replied: 'I honestly believe it is, but I do not like to swear positively to him.' Marshall Hall then shamed Headley as he held up a copy of the *Echo* – 'I have here a report of your today's evidence, printed before you were called.'

Marshall Hall delivered his most decisive attack on William Borking, manager of the South Quay Distillery, who stated Herbert and Mary Bennett had come into the snug attached to the distillery on the night of the murder. Borking was clearly a man with an eye to the main chance and had enjoyed the publicity the newspaper interviews and photographs had brought to his bar. Marshall Hall saw that Borking had taken his descriptions of the Bennetts from the newspaper accounts, for in cross-examination Borking could not qualify his description of the clothes Bennett was wearing in detail. Borking even claimed to have the very glasses used by the Bennetts locked in his safe, undoubtedly as 'trophies' for people to view – at a cost. He claimed he had been offered considerable sums of money for them. This whole matter could have been resolved if only fingerprint technology had been standard police procedure in 1900 (The first criminal conviction for murder obtained on fingerprint evidence in Britain was in the case of Albert and Alfred Stratton, who killed Mr and Mrs Farrow in the course of a robbery at Deptford in 1905).

Marshall Hall lanced a piece of spurious evidence, which despite earlier police searches had only come to light on 16 January, when Mrs Rudrum discovered a petticoat in her house marked in run ink with the name 'Bennet'. Seizing upon the spelling of the name he challenged Mrs Rudrum in cross-examination to tell the court how Mrs Bennett spelt her name, to which she replied: 'How should I know? She never spelt it.' To which Marshall Hall replied: 'How would you spell it?' Rudrum responded: 'B-e-n-n-e-t.' And then, after a pause, she added another 't'.

The most damning evidence against Bennett was the chain found in a portmanteau in his lodgings. The prosecution stated the chain was the one Mary had inherited from her grandmother, contending it was the same one to be seen in the photograph of Mrs Bennett and Ruby taken on the beach, as well as that worn by 'Mrs Hood' at the Rudrums. This, the prosecution argued, was a conclusive link between Herbert Bennett, Yarmouth, and the murder of his wife. Marshall Hall was having none of it. He pointed out that the style of chain in the photograph was different to the style found among Bennett's property. On the photograph, Hall argued that it was a rope chain of the 'Prince of Wales' pattern, whereas the chain found at Bennett's lodgings was of the chain type. Photographic experts were called and argued that the chain may have been of the link type, but it had been distorted to look like the rope type by the woman breathing as the photographic plate was exposed. Marshall Hall was convinced he had persuaded the jury of his opinion: in the event, evidence for and against the chain was inconclusive.

The final twist in the court case came in the form of sworn evidence given by Mr Sholto Douglas. Douglas – seen by many as a 'substantial citizen' – was proprietor of the London Fancy Box Company. He had given much thought to a chance encounter with a man he believed was Herbert Bennett on the late afternoon and evening of 22 September. Marshall Hall wondered at the suitability of this witness for the case: could he be believed at this late stage? Could he be mistaken? Marshall Hall asked Bennett if he recalled the meeting. He swore he did. Marshall Hall then asked Bennett to consider carefully if

Douglas should be called. To allow Bennett to consider the matter fully, he left a paper with two options: one to call Douglas, the other not to. Marshall Hall did not want a reply for two hours. The paper passed to the warder requested that Douglas be called to give his testimony.

Douglas had been taking a walk near Bexley when he met a man wearing a grey suit, who bore a strong resemblance to Bennett. The stranger walked with Douglas and asked him to have a drink with him. After a glass at the Tiger Inn, Douglas recalled that – as they stepped onto the street – the man said: 'By the way, a namesake of mine lives there.' He pointed to the sign-board over the shop, which read: 'F.K. Bennett, Shaving Saloon'. The time Douglas gave for his walk was between 5.15pm and about 7pm on Saturday 22 September 1900. The last train to Yarmouth left at 5pm. Sholto Douglas was a respectable citizen, he was unconnected to Bennett and had nothing to gain by lying – could he have been mistaken?

The trial lasted six days. Due to Bennett's track record of lying, Hall did not ask him to take the stand. He excused this by saying Bennett was 'too unreliable to put in the witness box', but as Marshall Hall's biographer Edward Marjoribanks puts it: 'from this abstention an overwhelming inference was drawn . . . if only Bennett could have gone into the box to corroborate. Such a powerful argument might well have caused the jury to doubt, and Bennett might have escaped.' Even so, Marshall Hall's summing-up speech was both eloquent and compelling – but it was not enough. Marshall Hall had suggested Mrs Bennett had fallen prey to 'a madman who, like Jack the Ripper and others of his class, had remained undetected and undiscovered' or 'some of the prowling brutes who haunted the shores at Yarmouth – some brute whose object was the lust and greed for gold'. This latter comment did not go without firm rebukes of such a libellous suggestion from the Yarmouth press. Lord Chief Justice Alverstone, presiding over this, his first murder trial, took over two hours in his summing-up. His tack was decidedly against Bennett. The jury retired at 6.35pm and within thirty-five minutes they reached an agreement, returning a verdict of 'Guilty'.

Appeals were lodged but all were refused. Bennett was returned to Norwich Prison to await execution. When all hope of a reprieve had passed, Bennett was visited in the condemned cell by various officials, such as the prison chaplain and the Governor, asking if he had any statement to make. He retorted curtly: 'No confession.'

Bennett went silently to his execution, carried out by father and son Public Executioner team James and Thomas Billington, on 21 March 1901. Even after the conviction Marshall Hall maintained his belief in Bennett's innocence. The eloquent defence he presented made others think twice about the guilt of Herbert Bennett.

There is a strange postscript to the case. When the black flag was hoisted to proclaim Bennett's execution at Norwich Prison, the flagstaff gave way and fell: an event construed by some as a divine sign of Bennett's innocence. Almost twelve years later, early on the morning of Monday 15 July 1912, the body of a young lady was discovered on Yarmouth's South Beach – the very same beach where Mary Jane Bennett had been murdered, but about 400yds further up and beyond the Nelson Monument. The victim had been strangled with a bootlace from one of her own shoes.

The woman's body had been discovered by William Smith and Daniel Docwra, out exercising a young horse. Shortly after 4am, the men had driven along South Parade; they went around the monument and were proceeding towards the harbour mouth when, about 300yds from the Nelson Monument, they saw the body of a woman stretched out on the sands about 6ft from the east side edge of the roadway. She was clearly dead and the men wasted no time in riding off to find a constable. At the Holkham Hotel at 4.35am they encountered Sergeant Herring, whom they drove to the spot post-haste. From a cursory examination it was plain she had been strangled, a shoelace tied tightly round the upper part of the throat, her stockings were tied tightly below to make doubly sure of her demise.

Sergeant Herring sent Mr Smith to the Police Station to fetch the Borough Chief Constable and Police Surgeon Dr Lettis (the same doctor who examined the body of Mary Bennett). The woman's chin bore scratch marks, probably caused by a struggle when the first ligature was applied to her throat. A considerable amount of blood was noted as having flowed from her nose. The body was recorded as lying 'in a most composed attitude' (no trace of struggle was marked in the sands around her), upon its back with the arms straight down by the sides, the legs straight out. Her hat was still on her head, secured by two long pins, and her clothes in such order that it did not imply a sexual crime (the post-mortem confirmed her as *virgo intacta* and found no indication of attempted rape). A closer examination revealed that the lace had been passed twice around the woman's neck and tied with a reef knot. The stockings were also secured with reef knots. The victim's legs and feet were bare: her shoes were nearby, one with the lace removed. A curious find was made by PC Dix, while travelling with the ambulance to remove the body to the mortuary. On the east side of the route, opposite Monument Road, he found a pair of lady's brown kid-gloves. They were later identified as the property of Dora Gray, but why they should be found some 280yds from her body remains a mystery. Theories abounded at the time and were explored by later criminologists, such as H.L. Adam, in *Murder by Persons Unknown* (Collins, 1929). Adam concluded the woman was not killed on the beach but simply dumped there.

The girl had not been reported missing, so the police decided to make the body presentable, photograph it, and circulate the picture with a description of the deceased. As a result the body was identified as that of 18-year-old

A contemporary artist's impression of how the body of Dora Gray appeared when discovered. *(Stewart P. Evans Archive)*

Dora May Gray, a boarding house day-girl, who lived with her two aunts, Miss Selina Eastick and Mrs Brooks, at the back of 10 Manby Road, off St Nicholas Road.

Police enquiries initially threw up a couple of suspects, both young men: one from Fakenham, whom she had met while he was on holiday, and who had recently written to her; and another who appeared on a photograph with Dora, which she had hidden behind her mirror – he was dressed in a white drill suit and sailing cap. Both men produced alibis for the night of the murder. The police also questioned the soldiers of the Rifle Brigade, who had been allowed out on passes from their encampment on the North Denes that night. Another leading clue was that Dora was known to guest frequently on the yachts of gentlemen who sailed out from the local yachting station. Dora had spent the last day of her life there. Hubert Baldry (aged thirteen), the son of the yacht station attendant, recognised Dora, and having not seen her for a while, asked her where she had been for so long? To which she replied: 'I have

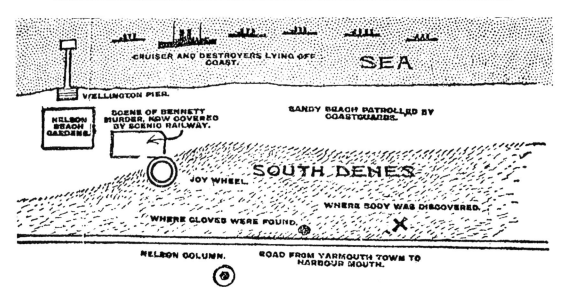

A map showing the locations where the bodies of Mary Bennett and Dora Gray were discovered. *(Stewart P. Evans Archive)*

been to Lowestoft with a gentleman.' She then went aboard the yacht *Medea*, from Wroxham, and stayed there for lunch and into the afternoon, when the yacht cast off at 4.30pm.

As Dora was leaving she saw young Hubert again and concluded her conversation by telling him she was 'going for a walk that night on the Drive with the gentleman she went to Lowestoft with'. Dora then went home, got changed, and was last seen alive at about 9.10pm by a female acquaintance named Miss Emily Blyth, who worked as an assistant at Mr W.H. Rowland's stall at 13 Marine Parade, next to the Steam Packet Hotel. Dora had spoken to her as she walked past the stall. She was seen to be in the company of a smart young gentleman. Miss Blyth described the man as 'young – about twenty – sturdily built, and about Dora's height (5ft 4ins). He was fair, clean-shaven and fresh featured, and was wearing a neat suit of grey tweed.' The couple passed by and were last seen heading in the direction of the South Beach. Emily Blyth concluded: 'They seemed to be in a very merry mood, laughing, talking and frolicking.'

On the Tuesday after the murder an unknown person erected a rough-hewn granite slab over the place where the murder was discovered. Upon the stone was written:

In memory of Dorothy Maud Gray. May she be revenged.
15 July

A sketch of the stone erected near where the body of Dora Gray
was found.

On a piece of paper spiked into the ground was written: 'Here the body
was discovered.' Another account stated that the words: 'Remember Mary
Bennett' also appeared on the stone.

At the inquest the Coroner summed up: 'There cannot be a doubt that she
was in the habit of going out and seeing young men, and possibly going with
young men above her station.' As to the identity of the murderer and his
motive, the Coroner concluded his summing-up to the jury with the following:
'The whole thing is a dark mystery, which I am afraid neither you nor I can
unravel.' The jury returned a verdict of wilful murder by person or persons
unknown.

The remains of Dora Gray were interred during a low-key service, under
the auspices of the Board of Guardians at Caister, after a simple service at
the cemetery chapel. The coffin of varnished elm had a black plate with gold
lettering:

Nothing in my hands I bring, DORA MAY GRAY, Died 15 July, Aged 18
years. Simply to thy cross I cling.

Because this was, in effect, a pauper's funeral, the coffin had been taken to
Caister by hearse, but no carriage was provided for the mourners: they had to
go on ahead by tram. As the sad little group left the chapel they were joined

FIGURES IN THE BEACH MYSTERY:—DORA GREY, THE MURDERED GIRL; TOP PICTURES, MESSRS DOCWRA AND SMITH, WHO FOUND THE BODY; BOTTOM PICTURES, DETECTIVE-INSPECTOR MOORE AND CHIEF-CONSTABLE PARKER.

A montage of the main characters involved in the Dora Gray murder. *(Stewart P. Evans Archive)* by four 'special correspondents' from the London press. A good number of wreaths were sent and two lady mourners dropped small posies of sweet peas on the coffin.

The postscript to this case was that a number of men came forward claiming they had committed the murder of Dora Gray. Typical of them was an unbalanced man named Alfred William Moorcroft from Plaistow, who, after asserting he was the man the police were searching for, was questioned by Superintendent Alfred Marden of the Essex Constabulary. His story was soon exposed as a fabrication. Moorcroft later claimed he had read so much about the crime that he eventually began to think he had committed it. He also stated that his mind had been affected by reading about the *Titanic* disaster. Another strange confession came from George Ward, in the October after Dora's murder. Ward was a 23-year-old farm labourer, who, like many who worked the land at harvest times, spent the rest of the year on fishing boats. Ward had gone to Litcham Police Station to give himself up as the murderer of Dora Gray. Brought before the magistrates it was noted that: 'He struck one as a man of not very bright intelligence as his face wore a dull and heavy and somewhat loutish look.' Ward was remanded pending further inquiries, which revealed he was not in Yarmouth at the time of the murder. The killer of Dora Gray was never identified, nor was any motive for her killing ever established. The murder of Dora Grey remains a tantalising mystery to this day.

6

VALENTINE'S TRAGEDY

Norwich 1903

February is, of course, the month in which St Valentine's Day is celebrated. It should be a day of romance, love and passion. But in 1903 the shine of the day was dulled by a tragic event that cast a pall over the city of Norwich and blackened the pages of the press.

Robert J. Read, proprietor of the St Swithin's Mill, Lower Westwick Street, was a kindly gentleman, who lived a quiet life with a small staff at his comfortable home, Rivington, situated on the right-hand side of Newmarket Road, leaving Norwich. Being a good and fair employer he easily retained staff for long periods. Among his employees was Ellen Baxter, who had been at the house for some six years. A well-liked girl of twenty-three, her employer freely stated he 'had implicit trust in her'. A short while after she joined the staff she met James Everitt Cook (aged twenty-eight) at a wedding. A native of Saxmundham, Cook was employed as a platelayer on the Great Eastern Railway. The two had a great time together, and giggled over his nickname of 'Valentine' – he was born on 14 February. They agreed to meet again and started walking out together. Paddling palms (holding hands) and laughing, they made a handsome couple, and by 1899 were planning to get married.

But when soldiers started marching to the South African War Cook joined their number, volunteering for the Royal Field Artillery. Ellen was proud of her soldier boy and waved him off to war with a tear in her eye. When he returned in 1902 Cook wanted to live closer to Ellen and lodged, on occasion, with Mrs Hipper on Melrose Road, just around the corner from Rivington. However, all was not well with the returned Gunner: the reality of war and its horrors having touched him. It seems James had met with a tragic accident. He had fallen from his horse, undergoing three operations and receiving prolonged hospital treatment. It is possible Cook was also suffering from what is diagnosed today as post-traumatic stress disorder. Friends saw Cook as a 'changed man' in body and mind, prone to irrational outbursts of anger and swings of mood brought on by frustration. Ellen sadly concluded that it was best they call off the marriage and end their engagement, but she was keen to point out she would always receive Cook as a friend.

At first this arrangement seemed to work. Cook would obey the conventions of the time, writing mannered letters to arrange occasional cordial visits, when they would take tea together and exchange pleasantries as friends. But as the months went by Cook's behaviour became more and more irrational. He began calling at Rivington unexpectedly, and Ellen became concerned for her job on account of his behaviour.

James 'Valentine' Cook, proudly wearing his South African War medal, walking out with Ellen Baxter.

On 11 February 1903 Cook arrived unannounced at Rivington. He was always personable and his injury received sympathy from the Read household. Cook had given up his job on the railway, his war injury having precluded him from such hard manual work. He asked Mrs Read to petition her husband on his behalf for a job at the mill. But Mr Read did not think his foreman required any extra hands at that time. After spending a pleasant evening together, Ellen broached the subject of his surprise visits. Keeping her approach light, she was confident the matter had been resolved satisfactorily and with minimal upset. Cook then asked if Ellen would care to go for a walk with him, and they set out at about 8.20pm. Ellen turned to bid her fellow servants a cheery 'farewell' as the couple set off. About 10.10pm, Ellen and Cook returned to the garden of Rivington and stood talking. Meanwhile, inside the house, Mr Read and his family were having supper. Suddenly, gunshots were heard coming from the area of the garden.

William Mack Fisher of Marlborough Road was cycling past Rivington with a companion, Mr Rich. Rich's light had malfunctioned near Mile End Road and they had both dismounted to attend to it when they heard the shots – one shot, quickly followed by another, with two more reports about a minute later. They thought that perhaps a local soldier had returned home

Newmarket Road, Norwich, *c.* 1905.

and was rattling off a few shot in the festivities, but something – described by Fisher as a 'flicker' – drew their attention to the driveway of Rivington. Not thinking about their own safety, Fisher and Rich bravely went to investigate. As they cautiously walked up the driveway, all was still. No voices, no footsteps could be heard – just a soft breeze gently rustling the foliage. About 15ft from the entrance gates they saw two prostrate bodies within 3 or 4ft of each other: a woman on the right side of the path and a man to the left, half on the path and half on the flower bed. A few more steps revealed the full horror of dead bodies bathed in the moonlight, pools of blood oozing across the ground. Both had been shot in the head. Fisher said to his companion: 'There's some deadly work been done here. If you stay I will ride hard for the police.' Rich stayed and Fisher got back on his bike and rode off at full pelt to alert the police.

As Fisher was leaving the drive some of the men who had been at supper in the house – namely Leonard Hill, Terence Read and Mr R.J. Read Jnr. – came rushing down the drive. They were soon joined by some of the servants, including Ethel Payne, who had been in the kitchen when she heard the shots. Entering the garden with some trepidation, she found some of the supper guests standing near the prostrate bodies, and was immediately sent back into the house. Meanwhile, the police were telephoned.

Mr Fisher did not have to bike far to Norwich City Police Headquarters, situated in the Guildhall, just off the Market Place. He first encountered

Norwich Guildhall, headquarters of Norwich City Police, 1903.

The gateway and drive to 'Rivington'.

Police Sergeant Varley, who after alerting the City Police Chief Constable, Edwin Francis Winch, clambered on his bicycle and sped off to the scene of the crime with Fisher.

On arrival at Rivington, Sergeant Varley ordered members of the distraught household staff back. He surveyed the scene and soon discovered the army revolver that had been used in the crime. As the Sergeant was noting down details, Chief Constable Winch and Dr Mills, the Police Surgeon, arrived in the police carriage. As the Doctor made his assessment the police ambulance was sent for. This vehicle was far removed from modern notions of an 'ambulance', being similar to a handcart with a detachable hood, rather like a pram, and propelled along by two policemen. The officers charged with ambulance duty viewed it as one of the worst jobs, as their charge could be anything from a vomiting and incapable drunk to a messy railway suicide. And so, by this contraption, the bodies of Ellen Baxter and James Cook were removed to the police mortuary on King Street.

The inquest was held at The Waterman pub on King Street, a short distance from the mortuary. Jurors left the warmth of the pub to enter the chilly morgue, there to view the bodies. They 'presented a shocking sight' and no doubt the inquest jury returned a lot paler, desiring to avail themselves of the strongest spirit the hostelry had to offer.

The facts of this tragic and horrible case were clear. The post-mortem revealed poor Ellen probably never knew what hit her. She had been shot in the back of the neck, near the base of the skull. It had taken three shots for Cook to kill himself. The first two shots – one just under the chin and one on the chin itself – only mangled his jaw, blowing out most of his teeth and blackening his face. Having failed with his first two shots, Cook fatally despatched himself with a shot through the eye. All that remained was a solid motive. There had been no indication of violent outbursts before, or during the couple's early evening walk. Perhaps Cook wanted to reinstate their engagement? Maybe he did not take kindly to a reprimand for his increasingly frequent unannounced visits to Ellen? Perhaps in of his outbursts he took the line 'if I cannot have you, no one can'? He took his motives to the grave. The inquest jury returned a verdict of wilful murder against Cook for the killing of Ellen Baxter and declared his death 'a suicide while in a state of unsound mind'.

7

A FORGOTTEN CAUSE CÉLÈBRE

Norwich 1905–6

In 1905 Norwich was a city 'on the up': trade and industry were flourishing and the horrific overcrowding of the city's courts and yards was being alleviated by the construction of terraced houses and tenements outside the city walls. To the south were the artisan suburbs, rows of bow-fronted terraces with large rooms, off Unthank Road. To the north, particularly in the area around the City station in North Heigham, there were the smaller, simpler terraces and tenements of the manual workers – many of them employed by, or their jobs relating to, the railway and goods sidings.

Living in the Heigham Street area meant living cheek-by-jowl with your neighbours. Everyone would have been 'in the same boat': of low wages, often struggling to make ends meet, and it was a society where everyone seemed to know everybody else's business – whether they liked it or not. Nostalgia can give such communities a rosy tinge, but times could be hard. Children were often dressed in hand-me-down clothes and some would not have possessed a pair of shoes. Despite healthy attendances at church and Nonconformist groups, one suspects most went for the social interaction rather than religious enlightenment. Many men, however, still found their main sources of entertainment in the numerous pubs. Meanwhile, arguments and domestic violence were, tragically, a familiar part of everyday life.

One such street was Railway Street. Numbered 1 to 29 it was one of several short row tenement streets, which with parallel Barker Street and Black Horse Street, ran off Heigham Street towards the cattle lairs of Norwich City station. At no. 29, the house at the end of the street, nearest the palings of the cattle pens, lived James Kowen (thirty-nine) with his wife Rosa (thirty-eight) and their two children Reginald (twelve) and Clifford (four). James was foreman cattle loader at the City station on 26s a week. In addition to this, Kowen worked in partnership with Albert Cooper in their own pony and trap business. In comparison to their neighbours, the Kowen family were doing well. The Kowens' house consisted of three rooms downstairs, bedrooms above, and privy plus horse and cart shed in the garden. James – known to

A typical Norwich street of terraced houses, *c.* 1905.

most as 'Jim' or 'Jimmy' Kowen – was a well-known character in the area. He had the reputation of being 'a bit of a dealer', being shrewd and frugal, and was a prime mover in the district's friendly societies. Rosa stayed at home to raise the children. The Kowens even had a woman, Maria Hastings, to do housework once a week.

The twenty-eighth of December 1905 had been much the same as any other day in the Kowen household. Mrs Mary Ann Tills, the next-door-neighbour, had seen Rosa go inside about 9pm, after a short conversation in which Rosa had told Tills she had to get cleaned up because her little boy had suffered a severe nosebleed. James Kowen returned from Albert Cooper's house on Barn Road shortly after 10pm (it was a six-minute walk between the properties). Ethel Tills, the daughter of the Kowens' neighbour, had been walked home by Mark Greenfield about midnight and noticed the Kowens' bedroom light was on. As Ethel prepared for bed she heard Mrs Kowen's voice calling, 'Fire!' Ethel raised the alarm in the Tills household. Her father, Alfred, rushed round to the Kowens', while her mother ran to summon help from another neighbour, army pensioner James Jeary. Samuel Grand, whose house almost faced the Kowens' from across the street, had also heard Mrs Kowen's cries for help. Rosa Kowen and her children were crying out for help from her bedroom window. Among her cries, Mrs Kowen was also heard to express concern for the whereabouts of her husband. Grand stated that she asked: 'Jimmy, where is he? Is he on the meadows or is he with Cooper?' Grand ran round the back of the Kowen house and discovered the living room on fire. He was met in the back yard by Alfred Tills. Grand returned to the front of the house and got Mrs Kowen to lower the children to him from the window, after throwing a bed and clothing out of the window. Rosa Kowen then lowered a cash tin out of the window into the care of Mrs Tills. Grand assisted Rosa's escape by leaning a sturdy plank against the window. As Mrs Kowen slid down it someone in the gathered crowd shouted: 'Where is Jimmy?' She replied: 'I heard him go out the back. I don't know whether he has gone out on the meadows.' Rosa Kowen then went with her children to Mrs Tills' house to recuperate.

In the meantime, Ethel Tills had run to summon a police constable – PC Gardiner – who had been on duty in Lower Westwick Street. He sent for the fire brigade, and on his arrival at 29 Railway Street, accompanied Grand to the rear of the house, where he discovered there was not only a fire in the sitting room grate but another blazing in the corner of the room. Grand

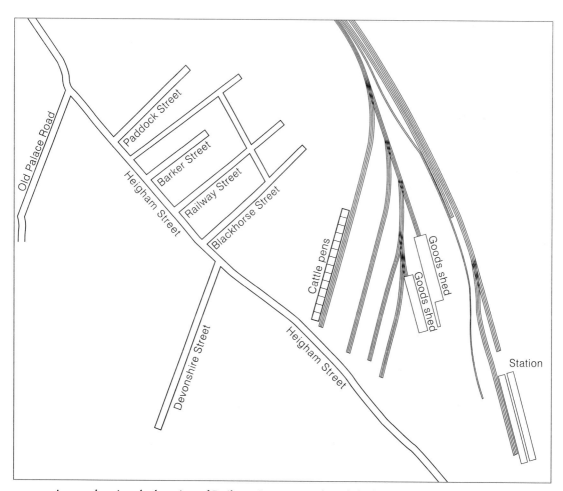

A map showing the location of Railway Street (now demolished).

opened the door and was immediately hit by the intensity of the fire, which singed his eyebrows and hair, causing him to retreat. PC Gardiner's attempt to enter was also foiled by the heat. But the indefatigable policeman soaked a handkerchief in water, placed it over his face, and managed to enter the room in a crouching position. Grand, joined by Jeary, followed the policeman and they managed to extinguish the fire in the corner of the room with a number of pails of water. They then discovered the body of a man lying halfway between the hearth and the incendiary fire. The face and clothes were so badly burned the figure was not immediately identifiable, but it was noted he had no collar and tie, and no boots on. When PC Gardiner caught hold of the shoulder to lift the body, the burnt clothes simply crumbled in his hands. Aided by Grand and Jeary, Gardiner placed his hands under the shoulders, and the body was lifted and removed outside. As Grand lifted the body he noticed the incongruous sight of a hammer on the mantelpiece.

Once outside, PC Gardiner shone his lamp upon the charred face of the body. Jeary recognised the blackened corpse and solemnly stated: 'That is Jimmy Kowen.' Dr Mills was summoned and soon confirmed the thoughts of all who had seen the body of James Kowen: that he had been killed and an attempt had been made to disguise the crime by setting his clothes on fire. As the body was carried outside Rosa was standing in the Tills' doorway with Jane Grand, whom she asked: 'Who is it?' Grand replied that she feared it might be 'Yankee' Edwards (another neighbour), to which Rosa replied, 'It's not Yankee, it's my husband. Yankee would not be at my house at this time of night.' Upon realising what she had said, the horror of the situation seemed to sink in and she ran over to the body. But she stopped short. The horror appeared to hit her – it was her husband and she cried to Mrs Tills: 'Never! Never! What shall I do?' A short while later Rosa, after a long period of silence, confided to her neighbour and friend Mrs Tills: 'If it wasn't for my husband it would never have happened.' It was to be the first of a number of ambiguous statements made by Rosa Kowen over the next few days.

Cursory examination of Kowen's head revealed two types of injury: sharp, deep cuts and 'rounded wounds' inflicted by a blunt instrument, indicating he had been attacked by two separate weapons.

The fire brigade arrived with the city's Chief Constable, E.F. Winch, close behind. The fire dealt with, the police – namely, Chief Constable Winch, Inspector High, Sergeant Goldsmith and PC Gardiner – set about investigating the scene of the fire. Much of the furniture in the living room was badly charred, piles of charred clothes were found where the body had lain and in the corner of the room, clearly these had been the fuel for the fire. Upon closer examination these piles of clothes were found to have been doused in paraffin oil. A pool of blood spread under the charred sofa and blood was spattered up the walls. Some of James Kowen's teeth – knocked out by the force of the hammer blows to his head – were also discovered on the floor.

The hammer was on the mantelpiece, despite having apparently been washed: it still had traces of blood discernible on the handle and over the head. Upon examination it was clear the hammer had been used with such force that the head of the tool was slightly sprung from the handle.

Chief Constable Winch proceeded to Mrs Tills' house to interview Rosa about the circumstances of the fire. He pointedly stated in his opening remarks at the inquest that although both the children were extremely upset, Rosa appeared 'calm and collected'. In the statement Winch took from Rosa, she stated she had retired to bed between 9.30pm and 10pm:

> I was awakened by my husband coming home. He came into the bedroom, took off his collar, tie and front . . . he said he had a pain in his stomach and would have to go to the closet. [When he got downstairs] he called up, 'there's a nice fire down here, I'll stop down and read.'

Rosa then claimed she drifted off to sleep but was woken by the sound of breaking glass and the smell of smoke: 'I went downstairs but could not get in the living room door on account of smoke.' She then collected the children and summoned help from the bedroom window. When asked what she thought may have happened to her husband, she said: 'My husband has had a pain in the chest lately, I wanted him to go to a doctor but he would not. He may have been reading and taken suddenly ill had then fell on to the fire.'

On the following day, while police conducted further investigations, Mrs Kowen received a number of visitors who came to bring their condolences. In every case, witnesses commented on Rosa being composed or 'ordinary', and primarily concerned with the benefits, pay-outs and pensions to which she was now entitled: one policy alone was due to pay out a lump sum of £100 plus a pension. Meanwhile, the police called in Mr Wilkinson, a commercial photographer from the Royal Arcade, who photographed the scene of the crime and conducted a detailed search of 29 Railway Street, along with its outbuildings. A large axe and a chopper were discovered in the coalhouse – both of which were bloodstained.

The body of James Kowen, having been rolled up in a large rug in the front room of 29 Railway Street, was removed later on the 29th to the mortuary, for a post-mortem examination conducted on the 30th. There were twenty-six discernible wounds to the head and throat. After comparison with the suspected weapons, these wounds were confirmed as being delivered by the hammer and chopper. The blow found on the upper part of the nose would have been enough to fell the man: the fatal blows had been delivered by the hammer to the centre of the forehead, causing a depressed fracture of the skull, the bone being driven into the brain by two blows.

House-to-house enquiries revealed that over the previous twelve months Jim and Rosa had been heard quarrelling on a regular basis – but then, few folks thought anything of regular cross words in this area. But it came to light that James Kowen had frequently argued with Rosa about her heavy drinking. Apparently, he had 'kept her short' – deliberately depriving her of money to prevent her buying whiskey and beer. As a consequence, Rosa took matters into her own hands, pawning items from the house to buy alcohol, and this led to further arguments. It seems Jimmy was known to 'knock her about' if Rosa got drunk.

Taken as a whole, the evidence and lack of emotion shown by Mrs Kowen suggested to many, including the police, that there was only one suspect for this crime – Rosa.

At 5.30pm on Saturday 29 December 1905, instructions were issued for Rosa to be 'taken to the detective offices on suspicion'. Cautioned that she was to be charged with the murder of her husband, she remained quiet and calm, replying: 'I did not plan to murder him, nor harm him in any way.' Brought before Norwich Guildhall magistrates in mid-January 1906, witnesses recounted the story of that fateful night, and the mutual and friendly society representatives gave statements as to the amount of insurance the death of James Kowen would bring his wife and family.

In her statement, Maria Hastings – the Kowens' old friend, who cleaned for them once a week – pulled no punches. Hastings stated Rosa frequently gave way to drink and she had seen Rosa strike her son Reggie across the face with a stick, drawing blood, while under its influence. She even claimed to have visited Rosa on the night of the murder, about 6pm. Rosa had 'taken a drink' and was claimed to have said: 'I am going to leave Jim tomorrow if I can get the money.' Her intention was to live with her sister in London. Noticing a broken door panel, Hastings asked how this had happened, and Rosa explained she had rowed with her husband the previous night. He had accused her of being drunk again and struck her arm with a cane: Rosa had responded by picking up a chair and throwing it at James: it missed, striking the door and smashing the panel.

When all evidence had been presented by the prosecution, and the formal charge of murder was requested to be heard at the County Assizes, Mrs Kowen still showed no emotion, but in a low voice replied: 'I reserve my defence; I will not call witnesses today.' She was then formally committed to trial at the Assizes, and 'taken down' unassisted from the dock.

The case of Rosa Kowen came to trial at the Norfolk Assizes in March 1906. The prosecution was led by Mr Horace Avory (later Lord Chief Justice Avory). Rosa was fortunate to have Mr Ernest Wild (the man later to become Sir Ernest Wild, Recorder of Norwich) to act in her defence. This brilliant young barrister had already acquired a reputation for defending what appeared to less able counsels as lost causes. By exploring issues raised where only circumstantial or lack of evidence was apparent, Wild confronted juries with robust, unanswerable questions of 'reasonable doubt', which could swing the verdict from guilty to acquittal – or at least cause a 'hung' jury, when a unanimous decision cannot be agreed.

At the time of Rosa's trial, Wild had already come to national prominence due to his successful defence of William Gardiner, a case popularly known as 'The Peasenhall Murder'. Gardiner, an upstanding member of the Peasenhall village community, had stood accused of the murder of Rose Annie Harsent (aged twenty-three), who had been found with her throat cut and her nightdress partially burned at the bottom of the stairs at Providence House, Peasenhall on 1 June 1902. Gardiner was a married man and much had been made of the alleged secret dalliances between Methodist choirmaster Gardiner and chorister Rose Harsent in and around the chapel. A letter arranging a secret assignation with an unnamed man was recovered from her room, and the wagging tongues of locals pronounced Gardiner number one suspect. Wild presented a case for Gardiner's defence that raised questions of doubt – based on the lack of tangible evidence – over Gardiner's presence at the scene of the crime. The jurors could not agree: eleven were for conviction, one

A rare image of forgotten cause célèbre Rosa Kowen.

Justice 'Long
John' Lawrence,
c. 1905

for acquittal. Tried again the following January, the jury still stood at eleven for, and one against. Consequently, the case was declared *nolle prosequi* – in effect the law gave up and Gardiner was set free on 29 January 1903.

Just like Gardiner, Rosa Kowen was to stand trial on two occasions, both hearings spreading over four days. Coincidentally, the Judge who officiated at Gardiner's trial – 'Long John' Lawrence – presided over Rosa Kowen's first hearing. At her trials, much circumstantial evidence was given concerning the quarrels between James and Rosa in the months before the murder, some of which was dismissed by Wild, and some by the Judge in his summing-up – on grounds that those giving such evidence bore grudges against Rosa.

Comment was made regarding Rosa's lack of emotion after the tragedy, but both the press and her defence countered that Rosa was so traumatised by the events, her emotions had not had a chance to come out yet. Wild played on the question of how such 'an atrocious and ingenious crime' could be perpetrated by a woman. Questions were explored regarding the downstairs door: no one could confirm or deny it had been bolted when entry to the house was made. With conflicting evidence of James's violence and 'stingy' behaviour towards Rosa, the only motive that remained for the murder was collection of the insurance money. Wild stated that, considering Rosa's circumstances, this motive was inadequate, and the Judge agreed in his summing-up. The case came down to the burden of proof.

Wild punched holes in the prosecution, based on the lack of blood found on Rosa's clothing and a purse of money being missing from James Kowen's effects (although the prosecution countered that the purse and any blood-stained clothes could have been burnt in the fire around the victim's body). Above all, Wild eloquently put forward the suggestion that it was possible for a criminal, as yet unidentified, who had knowledge of Kowen's hammer and chopper, and knew of his habit of returning late from his business partner's

Ernest Wild at the time of the trial.

house. Wild suggested that, having waited outside, the unknown assailant obtained entry by following James in, violently murdering him and stealing what money he could find, then started the fire to cover his tracks. With the seeds of doubt planted in the jury's mind they failed to agree and a retrial was ordered.

The new trial was set for the Summer Assizes of June 1906, by which time the local and national press reflected a groundswell of sympathy for 'the plight of Mrs Kowen'. Much the same evidence was presented at the second trial. Remaining impassive in the dock, flanked by two stern prison wardresses, the figure of Rosa Kowen made a pathetic sight. Crowds filled the public galleries to watch the proceedings and waited outside the prison and the Shirehall for the arrivals and departures of Mrs Kowen by prison van: some ladies even sprinkled rose petals in her path. On Saturday 16 June Mr Justice A.T. Lawrence delivered his summing-up, presenting each side of the case evenly. In his final remarks to the jury he said he would not:

> insult you by supposing any of you would flinch from the performance of your duty . . . If you come to the conclusion that you are convinced that the prisoner was guilty, then you must say she was guilty, however much you may dislike that duty. If, on the other hand, you are not satisfied as reasonable men that she was guilty then you should say so.

After a deliberation of two and a half hours the jury returned and stated they 'had no reasonable chance of agreeing on a verdict'. Judge Lawrence stated the trial would be adjourned to the next Assizes. There was a public outcry. Prevailing sentiments were clearly voiced on handbills circulated at the time, boldly headed with the name Rosa Kowen and emblazoned with the challenge: 'This woman has stood trial on two occasions, neither jury could agree, why should she be put through this hideous and demeaning experience again?'

As the days and weeks passed after the trial the hubbub of outrage died down until early July, when there was rumour of a *nolle prosequi* (no further prosecution) declaration being made in favour of Mrs Kowen. Pressmen made up the majority of the crowd that lingered in front of Norwich Prison, each one attempting to catch a glimpse of those in the carriages going in and out, seeking some confirmation of the decision. On Thursday 5 July 1906, Rosa's solicitor, Mr W.E. Keefe, told her privately in her cell that her release was imminent. The Governor, Major Fowler, announced the good news to her on receipt of the relevant papers from the Home Office the following morning. When Rosa left prison the announcement of her release had not been trumpeted by the press. As a consequence, only a few hardy souls and pressmen saw the shuttered cab containing Rosa, her father and Keefe leave the prison. The party proceeded directly to Thorpe station, boarding the

The Shirehall, Norwich, as it would have looked at the time of the trial of Rosa Kowen.

3.27pm train for London Liverpool Street. Not a soul seemed to recognise the party on the station and they left without incident.

On Wednesday 18 July 1906 Messrs Clowes & Nash, auctioneers, sold the 'relics of the Heigham Murder' at their midweek sale in the Norwich Corn Hall. Most of the articles mentioned in the case – with the exception of the weapons and the burnt frame of the couch, near which James Kowen had been discovered – had been handed back to the landlord by the police and were up for sale. Mixed with the other lots, Fred Nash the auctioneer did not make any allusion to the origin of the items, but they could hardly be missed, and many folks came just to look at the incongruous charred effects on offer. These constituted the contents of the Kowens' living room and included the smoke-damaged overmantel, fireguard, fender, chairs, table, gramophone, and even an enlarged photograph of James Kowen, which realised 6s on its own. Each item attracted more money than was expected – far more than any other fire-damaged items offered for sale in the past. One visitor drew particular attention: the Kowens' mongrel collie dog came to bid farewell to his late master's furniture. The dog was accompanied by, and had been taken under the wing of, the Kowens' old friend George 'Yankee' Edwards.

And so the final curtain fell on the case of the Heigham Murder and Rosa Kowen retreated into obscurity – well almost. In early February 1927 a few local newspapers, no doubt with eagle-eyed, long-serving staff, reported: 'The list for interments at Norwich Cemetery for last week, under the date of 4 February, included the name of Rosa Kowen (58).' The articles, accompanied by the reminiscences of PC Gardiner (by then promoted to Inspector Gardiner of Norwich City Police), revealed that shortly after her release Mrs Kowen was certified insane and removed to an asylum in Kent, after which she was transferred for the rest of her life to the Mental Hospital at Hellesdon, near Norwich.

8

THE CATTON HORROR

The beat of a country copper in the years before patrol vehicles and radios was often a cold and lonely duty. The policeman's cape or coat on a cold night didn't offer much protection, and his oil-burning bull's-eye lantern would be used far more as a hand warmer than for shining a light.

It was on a dark and gloomy night that Police Sergeant Slater was walking one of the loneliest stretches of his beat, along the greensward of the road between Catton and Hainford (part of the old main road between Norwich and Buxton Lammas) on Thursday 29 October 1908. This area was typical of Norfolk village surroundings – open fields, hedgerows, ditches and big old trees with creaking branches. About a quarter of a mile from the Lone Barn at Spixworth, where the nearest house on this section of the road was the home and forge of Mr Laws the village blacksmith (another quarter of a mile away), Slater noticed a figure lying in the grass. Checking his pocket watch, he saw it read 8.50pm. Thinking it a little early for straggling drunks, he paused to discern through the gloom what was afoot at this lonely spot. The upper body of the prostrate figure was on the grass verge, with its lower half lying in the ditch below a tall hedge. Something was not right. Turning on his lamp and casting a beam over the body, Sergeant Slater's worst fears were confirmed. It was the body of a young woman, fully clothed, but dead and almost cold. Her face and neck were gashed and masked in coagulating blood. Much of her clothing was likewise saturated.

The burly Sergeant Slater rushed back to the blacksmith's, called for Mr Laws, and sent him post-haste to the County Police Station in Norwich. By return, Inspector Roy and PC Sizeland were soon on the spot, and they set about searching the area for clues, especially a murder weapon. Dr Rees had been summoned from Magdalen Street in Norwich, but as he was absent, Dr Flack of 77 Magdalen Road was despatched on a bicycle. Unfortunately, he was misdirected, got on the wrong road, and only arrived at the murder scene at 10.50pm, just behind the cab of the first reporter on the scene. Dr Flack immediately set about his examination, working by the light of the reporter's cab lamps and the policeman's bull's-eye lantern.

The Doctor assayed the woman was about twenty years of age and 'presumed to be of the servant or working class'. She had been dead for about five hours, having received a horrible puncture wound so large and deep, it would admit a finger up to the knuckle, just above her collarbone. Worse still was the slash across her right cheek down to the corner of her mouth, which was thought to have been caused by a blunt knife (at the post-mortem a third wound was found on her back). Blood had 'flowed in streams' from these wounds. The upper part of her dress was sodden with it, and the white cotton gloves she had been wearing stained blood red. One report stated:

> The ghastliness of her appearance was heightened by the various little touches about her dress showing how carefully she had prepared herself for an evening out. Pathetically enough on her left breast was a little bunch of flowers.

Dr Flack, having completed his initial examination of the body, had it carefully placed on a cart and taken to the coach house of the Maid's Head Inn at Old Catton. Once ensconced at the coach house, the woman's pockets were searched. The contents – a packet of chocolates, a handkerchief and a purse containing 1s 7d – offered no clue to her identity. The newspapers echoed the concerns and questions asked by the police: who was the mystery woman? Where is the murder weapon? And most pressing of all, who had committed this horrible murder? In the papers of 30 October the police, despite having carried out extensive searches of the haystacks, ditches and buildings of the vicinity, freely admitted they had not found a single clue.

Their enquiries were not to last long. On the morning after the murder, William Arnold handed in a gent's cane and a lady's umbrella he had found the previous evening, as he was cycling home from

Photographed in the morning light after the crime, this is the spot where the body of Nellie Howard was discovered. Crowds of people came to view the scene and look for the bloodstains. Sergeant Slater is on the left.

his work as a farmer's assistant. Arnold had discovered these items about a quarter of a mile from the murder scene.

In the morning light a trail of blood was traced from the murder scene, over about 150yds, in the direction of Hainford. Five or six drops of blood were also found on the floor of the Maid's Head. Coincidentally, at the very pub to which the body had been removed, a man behaving in a suspicious manner, with blood on his hands and mud on his coat, had been for a drink that night. On hearing of the murder, landlady Mrs Emma Cullum reported her suspicions to Norwich Police. When she arrived she found the man she suspected in custody. He had given himself up and was being questioned by Inspector Ebbage.

It had happened shortly before at about 9.35am on Friday 30 October. A man walked into Norwich City Police Station and announced: 'You want to see me about that job last night'. He then gave himself up as the perpetrator of the murder. Although smartly dressed, his jacket, thigh and trousers were bloodstained, and his hands covered in scratches. Inspector Ebbage was called and cautioned the man, who said: 'Yes, I did it. What is done cannot be undone.' He gave his name as Horace Larter (aged nineteen) of Ber Street Gates in Norwich. He kept a mussel stall near the Agricultural Hall. Larter continued: 'I was there and happened to . . .' Larter stopped abruptly but then picked up his thread: 'Well, we had a little bit of nonsense. The old woman interfered. Her people I mean. In a fit of jealousy I suppose, I think that's the case.'

Larter was rambling and Inspector Ebbage had not been briefed about the previous night's events (the murder had been reported to, and handled by, Norfolk County Police, not Norwich City Police where Ebbage was based). Ebbage asked Larter what he meant, to which Larter, a little frustrated, replied: 'Murder charge at Hainford, Catton last night.' Larter continued: 'I have made a good job of it this time, I thought I would make a good job of it while I was about it.' Larter stated the girl he had murdered was his girlfriend, Nellie Howard. Inspector Ebbage then communicated with Norfolk County Police and handed the prisoner over to Detective Sergeant Fuller for further questioning. Inspector Roy went to see Larter in his cell at the County Police Station. Roy formally charged Larter with wilfully murdering 'Ellen Howard', to which Larter replied: 'Yes, that's all right, but it's Nellie Howard, not Ellen Howard.'

Independent of Larter's statement the murdered woman was formally identified later that morning as Eleanor Elizabeth Howard (aged nineteen), who lived at Hainford with her grandfather. It was also confirmed that she 'kept company' with Larter. Nellie, as she was known to most, had been employed in a few situations in Norwich as a general servant. During this time, about two years previously, she had made the acquaintance of Horace Larter. They had 'walked out' together, but eventually she left him on account of his excessive drinking. For the last eighteen months Nellie had left her employment

'X' marks the spot, the murder scene of the 'Catton Horror'.

in Norwich and returned to Hainford. She had seen this as a good time to break off her courtship with Larter. But he was not so easily dissuaded and had written frequent letters, asking forgiveness and to renew their relationship. But some of the letters were more forceful. In one he declared that if he caught her walking out with another man he would 'do for her'. In the weeks leading up to the murder Larter had redoubled his efforts by sending a fine box of chocolates, accompanied by a special plea that she might consent to see him again. More out of appeasement than desire, Nellie agreed to meet Larter and hear him out.

The inquest, held at the Maid's Head in Old Catton, opened on Monday 2 November. Villagers from Hainford, and from some distance around, travelled to hear the proceedings and catch a glimpse of Larter as he arrived. At the inquest the story of Horace and Nellie's last day together was related. Larter had been excited about the meeting and had told one of the cabmen near his stall that he was 'meeting his sweetheart' that afternoon. The cabby, George Howard, who knew them both, drove Horace and Nellie to Larter's home at the Gatehouse on Ber Street, stopping off on the way at the Norwich Arms, where Nellie was brought a glass of port wine in the cab. After a quick visit home Howard took the pair in his cab back to his rank on Agricultural Hall Plain. Howard was to state that he could see that although he was not drunk, Larter had been drinking before he met Nellie and was 'not properly sober'.

Around the corner from the cab rank, in front of the General Post Office, Herbert and Nellie caught a tram as far as the Whalebone at Catton, where they alighted in the direction of St Clement's Hill, and went into the sweetshop.

The tram driver also knew the two by sight and he too commented it was clear that Larter had been drinking. PC Poulter then took the stand. He had been placed in the County Police cell to take charge of Larter. After Inspector Roy had formally charged Larter he left the two alone and Larter voluntarily dictated a remarkable statement to PC Poulter:

I met her about five o'clock on Elm Hill. I had rather a job to get her to come with me. I took her for a cab drive round Norwich and went to the Norwich Arms in Ber Street. I treated her to two glasses of port and I also treated the cabman. I gave the man thre'pence to hold the horse time the cabman came inside with me. She would not come in the pub herself. I quite intended enjoying myself, as I knew she did not want me and I made up my mind to kill her. I had gone down to Pearsons the same morning and had bought a clasp knife, which I gave a shilling for. I felt as if I could have murdered anyone if I saw them speaking to her. I loved her so and this is all through love and jealousy. This is what hate and love will do. I intended her not to make a damn fool of me. After we had enjoyed ourselves in Norwich I walked along the road to take her home. It was about 6.00 when we started quarrelling. She told me she did not want me, and I said 'You shall not damn well have anyone else.' That was about 6.30 when I felt like a madman. I caught her by the throat with one hand and stabbed her twice with the other. Just as she was turning round, when I thought to walk away, I stabbed her again and she fell down and never spoke again. I stood by her quite five

A crowd awaits the outcome of the inquest on the body of poor Nellie Howard at the Maid's Head Inn, Catton, 2 November 1908.

Ber Street, Norwich, as Horace Larter would have known it.

minutes and I thought then I would do myself in. Then a change came over me. I knelt down in a pool of blood, which you will see by my trousers, and kissed her when she was dead. I lifted her head up to see if she was really dead and then I pinned my buttonhole on her and left her. Never mind, I suppose her soul is now in heaven. If it were not for her people this would never have happened. They have been saying things about me so I should not have her, and I think it's about the best thing I could have done. I have had this on my mind a long time.

A juror asked what sort of mind was Larter in when giving his statement, concluding: 'He seemed in very good mind?' The Coroner added: 'He seemed to be quite calm?' PC Poulter replied: 'Yes sir. But he did not seem to realise his actions.'

After committing the murder Larter had been to the Maid's Head at Catton. Serving him with a half-pint of ale, Mrs Cullum noticed the bloodstains and cuts to Larter's hands, which he claimed were caused by a fall from his bicycle. She recognised the man: he had been in her pub before, often in an 'excitable state'. After behaving in a disturbing manner and using 'very bad language' he was refused a second drink, and was advised he 'had better clear off'. Larter's sister, Florence Ludkin, stated that her brother had turned up at her house on Sprowston Road at about 7.30pm on the night of the murder. Larter asked: 'Can I come in? I'm a little boozy.' She advised him that her husband was asleep in bed but he could come in if he was quiet. After asking for a cup of tea, Larter said: 'I have cut my little finger. Can I wash it?' Florence looked at her brother's hands: they had several cuts and scratches upon them. She replied: 'No, you will mess the place up, let me do it for you.' She asked him to sit on the chair but he continued to move around the room in an agitated manner. He got up and walked to the door and said: 'Will you shake hands with me for the last time? I've killed Nellie.' He walked outside, turned around, and said: 'I shall give myself up to the first constable I come to.' And he walked off in the direction of Norwich. As Larter's sister recalled their final farewells, her brother looked back and shouted: 'Goodbye Florrie!' to which she replied: 'Goodbye Horrie. God bless you.' Upon which her testimony became too much, she broke down in tears, and in almost a state of collapse she had to be assisted out of the room. It was also noted that upon seeing this Larter remained unmoved.

Henry William Wright, the landlord of the Whalebone public house at Catton, testified that on the day in question his pub had been visited on three occasions by Larter. He had been in for a drink on his own in the early afternoon and had returned later accompanied by Miss Howard – she had a lemonade and barley, he had a whiskey. They stayed about five minutes. Later in the evening, between about 8pm and 8.30pm, Larter had returned on his own and in an 'excitable state'. He asked for a lemonade. Wright served him but noticed the cuts on his hands and the bloodstains on his clothes, which Larter, again, explained away as the result of falling off his bicycle. Mr Wright also noticed the clasp-knife, open with the blade showing, in Larter's pocket. Wright remarked it was probably through having his knife open that

Horace Larter and Nellie Howard from an illustration on the pamphlet sold to raise money for her headstone.

he sustained the cuts. Larter did not reply. Wright pressed Larter that he had better close the knife and put it away in his pocket. As Larter did so Wright noted it appeared to be an 'ordinary rough buck-handle clasp-knife with a rather long pointed blade'. Walter Parish, an assistant at Messrs Pearson's Cutlery Shop on Bedford Street, gave evidence that he recalled selling a single bladed clasp-knife with a spear point to Larter on the Wednesday or Thursday morning before the murder.

Medical evidence was presented by Dr Flack. He concluded that the fatal wound had been the 'v'-shaped puncture delivered above her collarbone – one side of the 'v' caused by the inward thrust of the blade, the other side from its exit. He also confirmed the girl had not been outraged, neither was she pregnant: 'Indeed there was every proof that she had led a proper and well-ordered life.' This statement probably implied that her hymen was found to be intact. This concluded the evidence. The Coroner asked the prisoner if he wished to make any statement. He replied in the negative. After due deliberation the jury returned a verdict of wilful murder against Larter and he was formally committed to trial for the murder of Nellie Howard. When he was informed of this Larter turned to the jury and in what was described as a clear and audacious voice said: 'Thank you gentlemen, one and all!'

The funeral of Nellie Howard was conducted on Wednesday 4 November. Her body had been laid in a coffin at her grandfather's house at Hainford. Shortly after 2pm the cortège of black-robed mourners led the procession along the village lanes to the church. The scene was made all the more tragic because the family could not afford carriages or even a horse-drawn hearse: so Nellie's coffin was pushed to the church with due reverence on a wheeled bier. At each of the crossroads on the way, small groups of villagers mustered to doff hats and pay their respects. Many joined with the walking mourners behind. Such was the general feeling of sympathy aroused by accounts of the case, many people attended the service from miles around.

When the walking mourners arrived there was hardly a seat left for them in the church. After the service, during which several people, including Nellie's grandfather, broke down and could go on no further, the cortège moved off to the cemetery, in the grounds of the old ruined church. Over 100 people followed at a respectful distance behind the bier and the chief mourners. As the sun set, Eleanor Elizabeth Howard was finally laid to rest. The Revd Barnard led the committal, concluded with the hymn 'Safe in the Arms of Jesus': so moved were those who attended that 'it was a pathetically weak and broken chorus that went up from the sorrowing throng'. Nellie's grave was covered in floral tributes from the surrounding parishes. Many people who attended were simple country folk who did not have enough money to buy expensive floral tributes: theirs were more personal and poignant, being simple bunches of flowers cut from their own gardens and laid by the grave.

The funeral of Nellie Howard at the old church graveyard, Hainford, 4 November 1908.

Horace Larter was brought up for trial at the Norfolk Winter Assizes on Wednesday 27 January 1909, before Mr Justice J.C. Lawrence. Quite a crowd thronged outside to catch a glimpse of Larter, and the public gallery inside was packed. For the Crown, Mr H.H. Lawless led the prosecution, and at the direction of the Judge, Mr A.L. Taylor acted for the defence. Larter, neatly dressed in a navy serge suit, walked briskly into the dock and upon being formally charged by the Clerk of the Court, replied with a plea of 'Guilty' in a firm and clear voice. A short exchange followed. Judge Lawrence asked:

'Do you know what you are pleading guilty to?'

Larter: 'Yes, my lord.'

Judge: 'Do you know the consequences?'

Larter: 'Yes, my lord.'

Judge: 'You wish to plead guilty?'

Larter: 'Yes, my lord.'

Justice Lawrence repeated the question and was given the same answer. He pointed out: 'There is a learned counsel who is kind enough to say he will defend you if you are tried. Under those circumstances do you wish to plead guilty? I don't wish to interfere. You know what you are doing.' Larter simply replied 'Pardon?' and the Judge repeated his offer. Larter then quickly responded: 'I would sooner plead guilty, my lord.'

Assured that Larter was happy to plead guilty, the Clerk of the Court asked if he had anything to say. Larter replied in the negative. The Judge was left with no option: he assumed the black cap and addressed the prisoner. After

Nellie Howard's grave
in Hainford old church
graveyard.

a brief résumé of the salient points of the case he summed up his views of the murder: 'Anything more cruel, more hard-hearted, it is hardly possible to conceive.' His Lordship then passed the sentence of death upon Horace Larter. It was noted that Larter's composure was apparently 'coldly indifferent'. After sentencing he walked with a firm tread from the dock. The case lasted a total of six minutes.

Ultimately, Larter was not to face the executioner. An appeal was lodged that brought his mental state into question, and Larter's sentence was commuted to life imprisonment at 'His Majesty's Pleasure' within the confines of the Broadmoor Criminal Lunatic Asylum.

9

THE KILLING OF
PC CHARLES ALGER

Gorleston 1909

To say Thomas Allen (aged fifty-six) was a disagreeable person is probably an understatement. A vermin destroyer by trade, he was also known to the Gorleston and County Police as a petty thief and poacher. Among his neighbours he was regarded as a quarrelsome and sullen man who regularly drank to excess, frequently rowed with and abused his wife, and paid little regard to his eleven children save an occasional belting.

On the afternoon of Wednesday 18 August 1909, Allen appeared worse for drink and one of the frequent arguments between Allen and his wife erupted in the backyard of their corner house at 12 St Andrew's Road, Gorleston. One of their neighbours, Mrs Agnes Maria Cox, who lived four doors away at no. 8, heard the shouting and a gunshot at about 4.15pm. Mrs Allen was crying out 'Murder!' and 'Help!' Mrs Cox ran from the back of her house in time to see Allen strike his wife with a rusty piece of a gun. Mrs Allen was already bleeding profusely from a gunshot wound to the lower part of her back. Bravely, Mrs Cox ran to Mrs Allen's aid and managed to pull the weasely man away from his wife, while Mrs Allen ran off to another neighbour's house, that of Mrs Gray. Allen wrenched himself away from Mrs Cox and pursued his wife to Mrs Gray's. The neighbour had wisely locked her door. The indefatigable Mrs Cox caught up with Allen again, got hold of him beneath his arms and dragged him three doors from Mrs Gray's house and tried to get the piece of gun out of his hand. Allen kept saying, 'It's all right, it's all right,' as he evaded its removal. Mrs Cox got hold of the piece and demanded: 'For God's sake, give it to me, I implore you.' Allen wrenched the weapon and himself free, stomped back to his house, and walked round the gable into the back garden.

Mrs Cox, fearing what Allen may do next, ran to the Police Station, which was situated some distance away in the High Street. Inspector Moore despatched PC 37 Charles Alger – who was then about to commence his beat by the riverside – to go back with Mrs Cox. Alger (aged thirty-seven) was an experienced policeman, with over fourteen years' service, and was well

Members of Gorleston Police, *c.* 1909. PC Alger is standing, second from right. *(Norfolk Constabulary Archive)*

known in Gorleston as a smartly turned out and popular copper. He was a family man with a wife and four children, all under ten years of age. Alger knew what sort of a man Allen was: he had had cause to remonstrate with him in the past, when he lived near the Constable on Trafalgar Road West. Mrs Cox left PC Alger at the middle crossroads on St Andrew's Road and returned to her own house. Alger strode over to the Allens' house and was met by Mrs Allen by the back passage. She told him what had happened and warned the Constable: 'Mind he has a gun!' To which Alger replied: 'Oh, has he?' Then he went round the house into the garden, where he encountered Allen. Seeing the arrival of the Constable, Allen asked him to 'come away from those old women' and go with him into the garden, where he would tell him all about it.

As Alger and Allen walked into the garden it started to rain. Witnesses stated that both men appeared to be talking amicably as they walked out into the yard and adjoining land at the end of the south side of St Andrew's Road, near the parish church, which Allen used as an allotment. Allen walked ahead and was seen to stop and stoop into a small straw and manure heap. Allen pulled out an old hammer-action shotgun, the stock of which had been broken off and the barrels shortened and filed down. Without any apparent warning, Allen fired almost point-blank at poor PC Alger – he didn't have a chance. Alger took the blast of the broad muzzle full on the right side of his head, face and throat, tearing a large hole in the neckband of his uniform, blasting off one set of his collar numbers, slashing open his jugular vein, and horribly mangling the features on the right side of his face. Alger staggered back about twenty paces before collapsing to the ground, mortally wounded. People who were sheltering after rain stopped play on the Recreation Ground heard the shot and saw Thomas Allen break and reload his sawn-off shotgun. Allen was heard to say: 'I have finished one, and there is another over here.'

Allen then excitedly walked towards the wooden palings of the Recreation Ground fence and started raving and shouting: 'Come on Smith, come out and show yourself, you're the man I want.' William Smith, an assistant gardener at the Recreation Ground had been subject to one of Allen's long-standing grudges, which had culminated in a fight the previous year. Smith had heard the shouts and put his head outside the shelter, where he had been standing out of the rain. Allen immediately discharged his shotgun but fortunately Smith withdrew his head just in time. Smith armed himself with a stout piece of wood and stood in a defensive position near the shelter door, fully expecting Allen to run onto the Rec and attack him. Allen did not cross over the palings: instead he walked down the fence to the entrance of the Rec and abused another man he said he had been searching for.

Mr George Warner, the head gardener of the Recreation Ground, had heard the shots and shouting. Followed by Mrs Popay and Miss Lancaster, he ran through a small gate in the north-east corner of the ground into Allen's garden in an attempt to calm him down and aid the stricken Constable, who was trying to get to his feet. Mrs Cox was watching and when she saw that

The collar number blown off Alger's tunic by the fatal shot.

A stone angel tends the sticken policeman on PC Alger's gravestone in Gorleston Cemetery.

Allen had spotted Warner running over, shouted: 'For God's sake keep out of the way, here he comes again!' But Warner did not stop, and as he stooped down to help the policeman, Allen turned around and ran back towards PC Alger and shot at him again. Alger fell to the ground without uttering a word, bleeding to death in a crumpled heap on a potato patch. Mr Warner caught some of the blast and was seriously wounded, staggering towards the fence, his head 'smothered in blood'. Some of the stray pellets also caused minor injuries to the legs and hands of the ladies who had followed him.

By this time scores of onlookers had been drawn to the scene and, on hearing the second shot, dived for cover or ran to summon assistance. Two young lads arrived at the Police Station about 4.40pm and gasped out news of the shooting to Inspector Moore, who left immediately with PCs Orford and Tink.

When Moore arrived on the scene a large crowd had gathered at the bottom of the road, but they had been held at bay by Allen prowling around with his shotgun. Tink was sent around the back of the garden to stalk Allen from behind, while Inspector Moore showed commendable courage by walking along the low fence facing the road. Seeing Allen about 50yds off, he hailed him with the words: 'You had better give in, Allen, I am going to have you . . . You had better surrender.' As he got closer he said: 'Come and give me that thing in your hand – you have done enough mischief already.' Inspector Moore continued walking and said: 'Come on, old Allen, I will not hurt you.' Allen appeared to refuse at first: he raised his arm to show the freshly reloaded weapon. With a spring, Moore grabbed Allen's wrist and pushed it onto the wall, wrenching the weapon from his grasp. PC Orford and Mr Cockrill assisted in pulling Allen over the fence and restraining him as Moore put the handcuffs on. Allen was then swiftly removed to the Police Station by cart.

Once at Gorleston Police Station, Allen was searched and a further two live cartridges were found in his pocket. He was later removed to Yarmouth Police Station, under the escort of PC Lee. The injured ladies, Mr Warner, and PC Alger, were all swiftly removed to the Cottage Hospital. Mr Warner was in a critical condition for most of the night but recovered. Alas, poor PC Alger breathed his last shortly after he arrived.

In the aftermath of the shooting, crowds of people came to see the scene of the tragedy, many of them taking away small souvenirs or photographing the planks and boxes with which the police had covered the bloodstains.

On the morning of Friday 20 August, Allen was taken from the police cells to appear before the magistrates. Newspapers recorded the scene in front of the Police Station, where a large crowd of men, women and children gathered in front, several deep, and along the way to the town hall door 'in the hope of being able to catch a glimpse of the accused man'. But they were to be disappointed, as the police anticipated public interest and removed Allen to the cells under the court an hour before the usual time. The public gallery was packed to such a degree that a number of privileged spectators were allowed in the body of the court. As the clock struck eleven Allen was escorted to the dock by PCs Chase and Chamberlin, who remained beside him throughout the proceedings, which were overseen by the Mayor as Chair of the Bench. When Allen

Thomas Allen, sketched from life, in the dock.

appeared, he was not the barrelling monster many were expecting. He made a pathetic figure in dock, described as 'an undersized and weak looking man'. He was pale, unkempt, and wore no collar. The surprise that such a specimen could have been the author of the crimes was quite palpable among those who observed the proceedings.

The formidable Mrs Cox, who had been first to tackle Allen, took the stand. She recounted her tale but was so distressed when she spoke of how PC Alger had died that she had to be removed from the witness box to regain her composure. After Mrs Cox gave her testimony Allen was asked if he had anything to say. Allen replied: 'I am a little hard of hearing, and if you don't speak up I can't hear you.' Inspector Moore, who was standing nearer the prisoner, relayed the Mayor's remarks. Allen replied in a voice little more than a mumble: 'I wish the Magistrates, if they possibly can, to have my case settled by an astrologer or planet reader, and they will say whether it is right or wrong.'

Allen was remanded for his case to be heard at the County Assizes. His case was brought before Justice Lawrence on Friday 29 October 1909. Questions had been raised regarding the sanity of Tom Allen. Dr Craig, physician for mental disease at Guy's Hospital had visited him on two consecutive days while he was in prison. After respectfully suggesting the evidence he was about to give may be unpleasant to ladies, the order was given for the galleries to be cleared of all women and children, and Dr Craig stated that Allen had claimed to have lived twenty-five years peaceably with his wife, but of late he had started noticing people 'coughing and whistling', and he believed this was some way of attracting his attention to the fact his wife was being unfaithful. He had hid himself in the coal cellar to watch, and later accused his wife openly. Mrs Allen strenuously denied the allegations.

Because his wife refused to admit to the infidelities, he had bought shot for his old gun, so he could shoot the men as they left his house. Allen had, in the Doctor's opinion, begun to suffer from insane delusions. As the Doctor pointed out, he was convinced that in Allen's mind he had no appreciation of the seriousness of the charges he was facing, and that Allen believed 'he had only to tell his story for it to be considered that he had done the proper thing.' The jury were not convinced. They found Allen guilty of murder and he was sentenced to death. An appeal was lodged and a reprieve granted, and Tom Allen spent the rest of his days in Broadmoor Criminal Lunatic Asylum.

10

THE LAST TO HANG IN NORFOLK

Old Catton & Dereham 1951

As a crime historian based in Norfolk I have found one of the most frequently asked questions is: 'When were the last hangings carried out in the county?' When I reply that they took place in 1951, invariably the answer is greeted with some surprise. All of the stories I have related so far took place beyond living memory: the cases I am about to relate are exceptions. In retelling these last stories I have not set out to rake over painful memories for the families involved, but to compile a book outlining some of the most notable Norfolk murders of the last 200 years. I feel it would be remiss of me not to include this chapter on the last two people to be executed in the county.

Dennis Moore was twenty-three. A typical city boy, he was born, raised and educated in the Norwich suburb of Old Catton, where he lived with his family on Woodcock Road. He had been courting 21-year-old Eileen Rose Emily Cullen since they first met on a trip to Great Yarmouth in June 1950. They soon became a devoted and loving couple, but when Eileen fell pregnant her father, Ronald Cullen, felt he had to speak with Moore and suggest he act responsibly. Moore readily agreed, the couple became engaged, and they set the date of 17 February 1951 to get married.

On Saturday 3 February, with the wedding a couple of weeks away and the baby due very soon, Dennis and Eileen went to the city to buy a wedding dress, borrowing some money from Dennis's father at his stall on the market along the way. After tea with Eileen's family they went to see Dr F.B. Champion at his surgery on Magdalen Road for a routine check-up on the progress of her pregnancy. The doctor was to go on record saying what a devoted couple they were.

When the couple returned to Old Catton they went for a walk up Oak Lane. In those days the city suburbs had a more rural feel to them, and they were not developed to the degree they are today. Oak Lane was, and in many ways remains, a leafy, tree-lined road, but in 1951 there was more open

Oak Lane, Catton. The cow shed where Eileen Cullen was murdered was near the tree line at the bottom of the field on the right.

pasture and fields around it. As they walked up the quiet lane in the darkness, Dennis held his fiancée close and asked her to accompany him to a secluded cattle shed a little way off the road. They were kissing and cuddling when Moore asked for sex. It was suggested by Moore in his statements that Eileen found this aspect of their relationship unpleasant, and she had refused him on a number of occasions before: combined with her condition at that time she refused him again. In his statement Moore was recorded as saying:

> We were kissing and cuddling . . . I put my arms around her and squeezed her to me very tightly. The next thing I realised she had fallen to the floor and her mouth was bleeding. I then realised I had hold of her throat and just couldn't leave go. After that I took her scarf, put two knots in it and tied it round her neck very tight. There was something in me and I just could not leave go. I loved her too much and I would not have hurt her for anything in the world.

Moore then ran home via the Park House pub where he bought a pack of cigarettes. Once home he grabbed a bread knife from the kitchen, went back to the shed and attempted to cut the dead girl's throat. Subsequent examination of her body revealed she had also suffered bruising to the right eye and had a large bruise on the back of her head.

After lingering back at the shed, perhaps for as long as 20 minutes, Moore went to a telephone box and called the police. Sergeant Byland received the call: the voice he heard was unclear and excitable, and thinking it was probably a stupid prank, Byland told Moore to 'Wait there' at the phone box and sent DC John McLennan and PC Herbert Lines to the location.

Moore was still there when they arrived, and after showing the officers to the scene of the crime he went quietly to the Police Station. At 11.30pm Detective Superintendent S.C. Kybird arrived at the cattle shed with Sergeant Sidell and other officers. It was there they saw the tragic body of Eileen Cullen. At 12.45am Superintendent Kybird caught up with Moore at Norfolk Police HQ. Kybird said: 'I have just seen the body of Eileen Cullen in a barn in a meadow at Old Catton. I am making enquiries regarding her death and I have cause to believe you know something about it.' Moore was then cautioned and made a full statement. Asked if he had anything else to add, Moore replied: 'No, sir'. But then, after a short pause, added quietly: 'I'm sorry.'

The inquest opened into the death of Eileen Cullen was held at the Woodman pub in Old Catton on 5 February. After Ronald Charles Cullen identified his daughter and gave a statement about the last time he saw her, the Coroner, Mr G.W. Barnard, adjourned the hearing until 25 June. Dennis Albert Reginald Moore was formally charged with murder at a special court before magistrate Mrs M.B. Jarrold, and held at the Norwich Divisional Office of Norfolk County Police on Monday 5 February 1951. When brought into court Moore immediately greeted his father and then took his place in the dock. He looked dishevelled, dressed in a crumpled pair of grey flannels, a grey pullover and no collar and tie. He appeared to listen intently to the charge and replied 'Correct' when he heard it.

In the early 1950s local newspapers did not feature the endless columns of detailed murder accounts their Victorian and Edwardian ancestors took for granted, but still, news of murders hit bold on the page tops. News of local murders spread like wildfire as ever: undoubtedly, talk of the crime was rife in Dereham as much as the rest of the county, so it is a curious coincidence that on the week immediately after another young man in Norfolk killed his pregnant sweetheart.

Twenty-five-year-old Alfred Reynolds and nineteen-year-old Ellen Ludkin both lived in East Dereham and had been going out for two and a half years. Her parents were not happy with the match but tolerated it for the sake of their daughter's happiness. In October 1950 Ellen fell pregnant and Alfred wanted to 'make an honest woman of her'. Ellen's parents said they would only allow the marriage if Reynolds got himself a job. This he promptly did – but then lost it in January 1951. This put a great strain on the relationship. But Ellen's parents were adamant: no job, no marriage. And fair enough – they only wanted a stable foundation for their daughter's future. But Reynolds was not going to accept that and was dreadfully upset when he was given this ultimatum. On Thursday 8 February 1951 Ellen and her mother Gladys were at their home of Park Farm Cottages. Reynolds came to the door at 2pm, Ellen's mother answered and he asked to speak to Ellen. He was invited in and he spoke with her for about twenty minutes and then they went out for a walk.

Gladys watched the couple from the window. She stated she saw Reynolds stray into a nearby field, where he picked up a 12-bore shotgun. The couple disappeared from view, but a few moments later Mrs Ludkin heard her daughter shout 'Alfie!' and a shot rang out. Mrs Ludkin ran out of her house, as did Mr Mayer, a neighbour who had also heard the shot. Both were held at bay by Reynolds, who then ran off. Once he had gone, Mrs Ludkin and Mr Mayer searched the area from which the shot came: there was a cycle shed and inside they found the dead body of Ellen Ludkin. The police were soon on the scene, and as a precaution, set roadblocks around Dereham and ordered buses across the county to be searched, in case Reynolds tried to flee. He had, in fact, simply returned home to 14 Northgate, where he confessed to his parents. Later he returned to the scene of the crime and gave himself up.

Reynolds was detained at Park Farm Cottages until Superintendent Kybird arrived. He was then removed to Dereham Police Station, where he was cautioned, and there he made his first statement. After the post-mortem Reynolds made a second statement. Reynolds claimed he had told Ellen that he was going to leave her forever. He claimed she said if he did that, she would throw herself out of her bedroom window. They went for a walk and Reynolds – by his own account – announced he was going to kill himself. He then asserted that Ellen suggested they make a suicide pact and that he should shoot her first. Reynolds claimed: 'The gun was standing with the butt on the ground . . . She pulled the gun up and pointed it in her face. She said "Goodbye darling, keep your promise."' Reynolds stated he had not intervened because he knew 'that was the only way out'. According to his testimony, he had put another live cartridge in the gun, which he intended to use on himself, but then changed his mind because he 'wanted people to know the truth why we had done it, especially my mother'. Reynolds was charged with murder at an occasional magistrates' court at Dereham before Mr H.W. Fox and Mr A.J. Myhill on 9 February.

The inquest into the death of Ellen Ludkin was opened on Friday 9 February, at Dereham Police Station, by District Coroner Mr L.H. Allwood. Evidence of identification of the body was given by Ellen's father, Mr William Ludkin, and Dr N.E.D. Cartledge gave his opinion that death was due to a gunshot wound to the face at close range. Death had been instantaneous. The inquest was adjourned until 16 June.

On 17 February Moore and Reynolds were brought separately before the magistrates at Taverham. When Reynolds was informed he was to be remanded he simply replied: 'Right you are.' James Hipwell, who appeared for Moore, said he had no objection to the remand and had no applications to make. Moore and Reynolds were now set to appear before the next session of the Norfolk and Norwich Assizes.

Moore appeared on trial first, before the presiding Judge, Mr Justice Parker. The trial opened on 31 May and ran until 1 June. Moore's defence counsel were F.T. Alpe and Michael Havers (instructed by Messrs Russell Steward, Stevens & Hipwell). They contended that although Moore undoubtedly committed the murder, he was 'labouring under such a defect of reason as not to know the nature and quality of the act he was doing'. Evidence of Moore's temper was given by former girlfriend Irene Hambling, who had gone out with Moore in 1949. She stated that Moore had attempted to strangle her after a quarrel. She agreed it was not a serious attack but Moore apparently did not remember what had happened until she told him about it afterwards.

Robert Riches of West Earlham also came forward. About four years previously he had done National Service with Moore and recalled an incident when they were stationed at Colchester. Moore started wrestling with another man named Baxter. It started as a joke, but as Riches pointed out: 'In my opinion he would have killed the boy if I had not stopped it . . . He had got excited and got hold of the boy's throat.' Dr John V. Norris, consultant psychiatrist to the East Anglian Regional Health Board, stated he had seen Moore on four separate occasions while he was in prison: 'He had a completely unreasoned jealousy of his potential father-in-law. I think that jealousy was based on a further statement he made that his advances to the deceased girl were sometimes repellent to her.' Dr Norris went on to state that such obsessions were 'ruminative' and that 'A person under the influence of such a rage might well commit an act and not know what he was doing at the time.' Dr W.J. McCulley, Medical Superintendent at St Andrews Hospital, Thorpe, did not feel that Moore would have absolutely no knowledge of what wrong he was doing, but he was clear that Moore was prone to fits of temper and violence. He said Moore was: 'immature, unstable and liable to impulsive conduct accompanied by outbursts of explosive rage.' However. Dr J.C.M. Mathieson, the Chief Medical Officer of Brixton Prison, and Dr B.M. Tracey, Medical Officer for Norwich Prison, both expressed their view that Moore was not suffering from any disease of the mind.

In his summing-up, Mr Alpe, for the defence, respectfully and eloquently challenged the jury to consider if Dennis Moore was really responsible for his actions. Could a man so clearly in love with his fiancée, two weeks away from his marriage, really turn around and murder her if he was in a sound state of mind? He pointed out the scarf tied around Eileen's neck had been connected in Moore's mind 'with a murder he saw on the pictures . . . What incredible behaviour for a normal man.' Mr John Flowers of the prosecution emphasised Moore's temper, which he displayed when he could not get what he wanted.

He contended that Moore 'had killed his fiancée but in this imperfect world many people had killed the person they loved in passion. Within the meaning of the law this behaviour was miles and miles away from insanity.' The jury retired for fifty minutes and returned a verdict of 'Guilty' and Dennis Moore faced a death sentence. An appeal was immediately lodged.

On 4 June Mr Justice Parker presided over the second trial for murder, that of Alfred George Reynolds. Mr Gerald Howard KC and Mr Garth Moore led the prosecution and Montague Berryman KC and Mr Tudor Evans acted for the defence. The case was heard in one day. The pivotal moment came with the evidence presented by firearms experts. Reynolds and the experts – both medical and ballistic – agreed the gun had been discharged about 6 to 9ins from Ellen's eye. The gun measured 36ins. Considering the distance at which it was discharged, it meant the trigger would have to have been about 42ins from her eye. The maximum distance between the girl's right eye and the tip of her forefinger was 34ins, making it physically impossible for the girl to have reached the trigger and fired the gun at herself in that position.

Alfred Reynolds' father testified his son had threatened suicide in the past and had suffered dreadful head pains and nightmares for years: this latter comment was later endorsed by Dr Cartledge. Detective Sergeant Burton pointed out that while interviewing Reynolds his mind had constantly been occupied with thoughts of Ellen: he wanted to be with her and he wanted to go back to the body. In letters from prison he had reiterated his desire to be with her and had requested photos of her grave. His mental state had to be questioned. Psychiatrist, Dr J.V. Morris stated he believed Reynolds' mental age to be about twelve years, qualifying his view with the observation that Reynolds 'was not a mental defective, but was not far removed in intelligence from being one'. In cross-examination, however, Dr Morris could not state Reynolds had a diseased mind. Dr Mathieson, the Chief Medical Officer of Brixton Prison, concurred with Morris that Reynolds was not suffering from a diseased mind and felt Reynolds had the 'emotions of a man of twenty-four controlled by the mentality of a boy of twelve'.

After the summings-up by learned counsels and the Judge, the jury retired and deliberated for forty minutes (newspapers took pains to point out the jury included two women). The verdict they returned was that of 'Guilty'. Asked if he had anything to say as to why the sentence of death should not be passed upon him, Reynolds smiled at the Judge and said: 'No, there is nothing I want to say. I thank you very much at any rate.'

Appeals for both Reynolds and Moore were lodged and brought before the Lord Chief Justice (Lord Goddard) in the Court of Criminal Appeal on Monday 2 July 1951. The appeals were heard separately; each lasted almost exactly five minutes. Mr Havers spoke for Moore, arguing that he should have been found insane. The Lord Chief Justice did not feel there was sufficient evidence for insanity and pointed to the experts for the Crown, who had stated they could find no trace of insanity. The Lord Chief Justice expressed the view that the jury at the trial had been given a complete and careful summing-up and had not found the appellant insane. The appeal was dismissed but Moore's father never gave up hope and organised a petition to the Home Secretary for a reprieve. This failed too.

Reynolds was escorted into the same dock immediately after Moore had left. Mr Montague Berryman stated Reynolds' defence was also insanity. He went on to say Reynolds now had a new story: that the whole thing was an accident. Berryman continued: 'Although I have considered the matter, I can say nothing to assist the appellant in regard to it.' Lord Goddard stated, having considered the way the case was presented at the trial, it was impossible for the court to interfere: 'It was a clear case of murder'. Reynolds had given the story of the suicide pact at his trial and made no allusion to any accident. The appeal was dismissed and the date for the execution of Moore and Reynolds was set for Thursday 19 July 1951.

The executions were to be conducted under the direction of Britain's 'No. 1' Executioner, Albert Pierrepoint, with assistant Syd Dernley appointed as 'No. 2 Executioner' in respect of Moore, with assistants Harry Allen and Les Stewart. Dernley was responsible for all the execution chamber duties for Moore, but as this was to be a double execution, with the condemned men hanged side by side on Norwich prison's large double drop gallows, the ultimate duty of pushing the lever to release the trapdoors was the responsibility of the 'No. 1' – Albert Pierrepoint.

Dernley recalled in his memoirs that he was pleased to have the presence of Chief Executioner Pierrepoint at this execution. Ever since the 'Goodale Mess' (see chapter 4) Norwich had been stigmatised as the 'graveyard of hangmen'. Dernley's last experience had not gone any further to negate that belief. The last man executed at Norwich had been murderer Norman Goldthorpe. Both of the senior, experienced hangmen (Albert Pierrepoint and Steve Wade) had been engaged for a job in Scotland, leaving Harry Kirk, an experienced assistant, to carry out the execution with Syd Dernley employed as his second. Everything seemed to have been planned and set up properly. Goldthorpe was launched through the trap, but as Syd recalled: 'From the pit came a snort . . . and then another snort . . . and another and another . . . It's gone wrong! Christ, he's still

Albert Pierrepoint, Britain's 'No. 1' public executioner, oversaw the last executions carried out in Norfolk.

Memorandum of Conditions to which any Person acting as Assistant Executioner is required to conform.

────────────

(An Assistant Executioner will not be employed by the Governor without the concurrence of the High Sheriff.)

────────────

1. An Assistant Executioner is engaged, with the concurrence of the High Sheriff, by the Governor of the prison at which the execution is to take place, and is required to conform with any instructions he may receive from or on behalf of the High Sheriff in connection with any execution for which he may be engaged.

2. A list of persons competent for the office of Assistant Executioner is in the possession of High Sheriffs and Governors ; it is therefore unnecessary for any person to make application for employment in connection with an execution, and such application will be regarded as objectionable conduct and may lead to the removal of the applicant's name from the list.

3. Any person engaged as an Assistant Executioner will report himself at the prison at which an execution for which he has been engaged is to take place not later than 4 o'clock on the afternoon preceding the day of execution.

4. He is required to remain in the prison from the time of his arrival until the completion of the execution and until permission is given him to leave.

5. During the time he remains in the prison he will be provided with lodging and maintenance on an approved scale.

6. He should avoid attracting public attention in going to and from the prison ; he should clearly understand that his conduct and general behaviour must be respectable and discreet, not only at the place and time of the execution, but before and subsequently ; in particular he must not give to any person particulars on the subject of his duty for publication.

7. His remuneration will be £1 11s. 6d. for the performance of the duty required of him, to which will be added £1 11s. 6d. if his conduct and behaviour have been satisfactory. The latter part of the fee will not be payable until a fortnight after the execution has taken place.

8. Record will be kept of his conduct and efficiency on each occasion of his being employed, and this record will be at the disposal of any Governor who may have to engage an assistant executioner.

9. The name of any person who does not give satisfaction, or whose conduct is in any way objectionable, so as to cast discredit on himself, either in connection with the duties or otherwise, will be removed from the list.

10. The apparatus approved for use at executions will be provided at the prison. No part of it may be removed from the prison, and no apparatus other than approved apparatus must be used in connection with any execution.

11. The Assistant Executioner will give such information, or make such record of the occurrences as the Governor of the prison may require.

────────────

(C3191) 100 6/51

A copy of the Assistant Executioner's instructions issued to Syd Dernley for the execution of Moore and Reynolds.

A typical condemned cell.

alive.' The sound, rather like snoring, continued to emanate from under the hood. The Governor was horrified 'and the little Under-Sheriff had gone from ruddy red to green'. They rushed into the pit beneath the trap, Goldthorpe's shirt was ripped open, the Surgeon applied his stethoscope and to everyone's relief confirmed Goldthorpe was dead.

Upon a closer examination it was found the rope had not pulled tight; a small gather of the cloth hood had jammed fast in the eyelet, prohibiting the rope from tightening fully at the crucial point at the nadir of the drop. It could have happened to anyone, but Syd did not see Harry Kirk at another execution.

Arriving on the afternoon before the execution of Moore and Reynolds, the executioners and assistants took up their lodgings in an apartment – curiously and uniquely for Norwich Prison – above the condemned cell. Pierrepoint observed the two men at exercise and worked out their drops according to the Home Office approved 'Table of Drops' with a little of his vast experience thrown in. The condemned men were in separate cells; one in the usual condemned cell, and the other in a cell almost opposite. The executioners and assistants worked as quietly as possible, testing the trapdoors and rigging the nooses, because the execution chamber was directly next door (the doorway hidden by a cupboard, which only gave up its secret when it was opened to allow the condemned, executioners, warders and officials through on the morning of the execution). Even with two men on the gallows trap, it was unusual for an execution under Pierrepoint's direction to last more than twenty-five seconds from the moment the cell door opened to the condemned falling through the trap. Pierrepoint was even known to have started a cigar before the execution, left it in an ashtray, and been able to return to enjoy the rest of it as the bodies hung for the regulation hour.

Mindful of the spectre of the 'Goodale Mess' and his last experience of hanging a single condemned man at Norwich, Syd Dernley recorded the execution of Moore and Reynolds in his memoirs as 'a completely unremarkable execution, about which I was extremely thankful, as no doubt were the prison authorities at Norwich.'

SELECT
BIBLIOGRAPHY

Abbott, Geoffrey, *William Calcraft – Executioner Extra-Ordinaire*, Barming, 2004

Anon., *Narrative and Trial of James Blomfield Rush*, Norwich, 1849

Anon., *A Full Report of the Trial of James Blomfield Rush* (Clarke's Edition), London, 1849

Atholl, Justin, *Shadow of the Gallows*, London, 1954

——, *The Reluctant Hangman*, London, 1956

Berry, James, *My Experiences as an Executioner*, London, 1892

Brend, William A., *A Handbook of Medical Jurisprudence and Toxicology*, London, 1919

Butcher, Brian David, *'A Movable Rambling Police': An Official History of Policing in Norfolk*, Norwich, 1989

Capon, Paul, *The Great Yarmouth Mystery*, London, 1965

Chapman, Pauline, *Madame Tussaud's Chamber of Horrors*, London, 1984

Church, Robert, *Murder in East Anglia* (new edition), London, 1993

——, *More Murder in East Anglia*, London, 1990

Dernley, Syd and Newman, David, *The Hangman's Tale*, London, 1990

Eddleston. John J., *The Encyclopaedia of Executions*, London, 2002

Evans, Stewart P., *Executioner: The Chronicles of James Berry Victorian Hangman*, Stroud, 2004

Fielding, Steve, *The Hangman's Record* (vol. I 1868–99) Beckenham, 1994

Griffiths, Major Arthur, *Mysteries of Police and Crime* (special edition), London, 1920

Lambton, Arthur, *Echoes of Causes Célèbres*, London, 1931

Mackie, Charles, *Norfolk Annals*, Norwich, 1901

Morson, Maurice, *A Force Remembered: The Illustrated History of the Norwich City Police 1836–1967*, Derby, 2000

Pierrepoint, Albert, *Executioner Pierrepoint*, London, 1974

Teignmouth Shore, W. (ed.) *Crime and Its Detection*, London, 1932

——, *Trial of James Blomfield Rush*, Glasgow, 1928

Smith-Hughes, Jack, *Unfair Comment: Upon Some Victorian Murder Trials*, London, 1951

Storey, Neil R., *A Grim Almanac of Norfolk*, Stroud, 2003

Wallace, Edgar (intro. by), *The Trial of Herbert John Bennett*, London, 1929

NEWSPAPERS AND JOURNALS

Cambridge Chronicle
Cambridge Independent Press
East Anglian Magazine
Eastern Counties Collectanea
Eastern Daily Press
Evening News
Family Tree Magazine
Famous Crimes
Illustrated London News
Illustrated Police News
News of the World
Norfolk & Suffolk Notes & Queries
Norfolk Chronicle

Norfolk Chronicle and Norwich Gazette
Norfolk Fair
Norfolk Journal & East Anglian Life
Norwich Mercury
Penny Illustrated Paper
Police Gazette
Reynolds News
The Criminologist
The Strand Magazine
The Tablet
The Times
Yarmouth Mercury

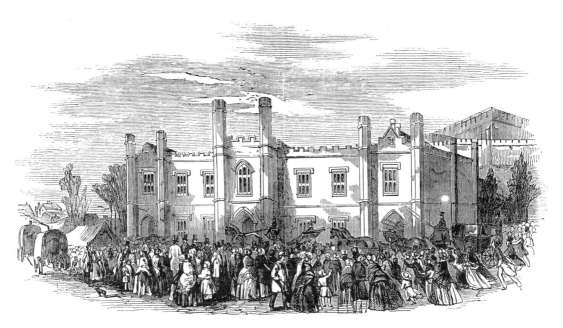

The crowds gather outside the Norwich Shirehall for a glimpse of some of the characters involved in the Stanfield Hall murder trial of 1849.

INDEX